POINTS OF CHURCH LAW

POINTS OF CHURCH LAW

AND OTHER WRITINGS ILLUSTRATIVE OF THE

LAW OF THE CHURCH

BY

CLEMENT Y. STURGE, M.A.

BARRISTER-AT-LAW, OF THE INNER TEMPLE

WIPF & STOCK · Eugene, Oregon

Wipf and Stock Publishers
199 W 8th Ave, Suite 3
Eugene, OR 97401

Points of Church Law
And Other Writings Illustrative of the Law of the Church
By Sturge, Clement Y.
ISBN 13: 978-1-5326-4297-5
Publication date 11/9/2017
Previously published by Macmillan and Co., 1907

PREFACE

A word of explanation is due for what may seem the temerity of reprinting and publishing in a connected form matters so diverse and incongruous as have been brought together in this little volume.

The "Points of Church Law" appeared, in answer to clerical correspondents, in the *Guardian* for the years 1900—3. They deal, for the most part, with points of law in connection with parochial administration, which are continually arising, and causing doubt and difficulty to the clergy, churchwardens, and others in the performance of their duties. It is hoped that, collected under headings of the points that most frequently arise, they may be found serviceable to the clergy, and even to lawyers. They claim no higher merit than that of bringing together in a convenient form the principal authorities on each subject treated. The references to cases have been given in a more extended form than is usual, as the book is designed to meet the needs of persons who are unfamiliar with the abbreviations in use among lawyers.

The summary of the arguments in Dr. Gore's case in 1903 is also a reprint from the *Guardian*. The case will, of course, be found more fully reported in the pages of the Law Reports, and the columns of the *Times*. But it was thought that, in a case so complicated and certain to become historical, there might be room for a more popular account compiled at the time with considerable care from an official copy of the shorthand notes. The arguments have been closely followed, but for references to the authorities cited in the case the reader is referred to the reports above mentioned.

The republication of two articles on the constitutional position of the Church of England in relation to Parliament and the Privy Council, and the Summary of the principal Judgments in matters relating to Ritual during the last sixty years, which originally appeared in a "Westminster Popular" entitled "The Crisis in the Church" in October, 1899, needs no apology at a time when, by the publication of the Evidence and Report of the Royal Commission on Ecclesiastical Discipline, public attention is once more drawn to the constitution of the supreme appellate Court in ecclesiastical causes, and to the recorded results of its deliberations on the questions which have come before it. It is hoped that the articles may assist those who are not experts in ecclesiastical jurisprudence in forming an opinion on the controversial points at issue, and that the Summary of Judgments may be found useful by students and others whom duty or interest may lead to explore the tangled paths of ecclesiastical litigation. Since 1877 there has been no judgment relating to the Ornaments of the *Minister*, with the exception of a case in the Court of Chancery (1891) and Court of Appeal (1896), in which the legality of the black gown in preaching came in question; but the list of those relating to the Ornaments of the *Church* has been enlarged and brought up to date.

In the Appendix will be found an historical and liturgical account of the Coronation of King Edward the Seventh and Queen Alexandra, reprinted with a few additions and corrections from the *Westminster Gazette* of August 11, 1902, for much valuable assistance in compiling which my grateful thanks are due to the present Dean of Westminster. It is hoped that it may be useful to liturgical students in the future.

I gladly acknowledge the kindness of the proprietors of the *Guardian* and the *Westminster Gazette* in allowing me to republish the reports and articles respectively contributed to their columns.

C. Y. S.

15, OLD SQUARE, LINCOLN'S INN.
April, 1907.

CONTENTS

I. POINTS OF CHURCH LAW.

	PAGE
Baptism	1
1. Omissions in Baptismal Register	1
2. Error in Name at Baptism	3
3. Registration of Baptisms by Laywomen	4
4. Burial of Unbaptised Children	5
Marriage	5
1. Banns of Marriage and Time of Publication	5
2. Residence for Banns of Marriage	9
3. Sunday Weddings	10
4. Time of Celebrating Marriage	11
5. Marriage between Cousins	12
Burial	14
1. Burial Fees: Incumbent's Power over Churchyard	14
2. Rights of Burial in more Parishes than one: Fees to whom Payable	17
3. Burial of Non-Parishioners	19
Vestries	20
1. Vestry Meetings	20
2. Vicar's Right to Vote at Vestry Meetings	21
3. Procedure at Vestry Meetings	22
4. Polls at Vestry Meetings	23
Churchwardens	26
1. Who may be Churchwardens	26
2. Lodgers as Churchwardens	28
3. Liability of Churchwardens	29
4. Remedies against Churchwardens	34
5. Re-admission of Churchwardens continuing in Office and Payment of Fees	35
6. Custody and Distribution of Alms	36
Churchyards	37
1. Timber in Churchyards	37
2. Lay-Rector's Rights over Churchyards	40
3. The Rating of Churchyards	42
4. Care of Churchyards	42

CONTENTS

	PAGE
Easter Offerings and Visitation Fees	44
1. Recovery of Easter Offerings	44
2. Easter Offerings and Income Tax	46
3. Fees at Archidiaconal Visitations	47
General	49
1. Rights of Lay-Rector to Seats in Chancel . .	49
2. Spiritual Oversight of an Orphanage	50
3. Status of Perpetual Curates	53
4. Status of Curates	55
5. Payment of Parish Clerk	56
6. Payment of Tithes by One Vicar to Another . .	57
7. Transmission of Copies of Parochial Registers . .	59
8. Repair of Family Tomb in a Churchyard . . .	59
9. Fees for Monuments in Churches	61

II. THE CONFIRMATION OF THE BISHOP-ELECT OF WORCESTER : Summary of the Arguments 64

III. IN DEFENCE OF THE CHURCH: From a Legal Standpoint 89
  I. THE CHURCH AND PARLIAMENT 89
  II. THE CHURCH AND THE PRIVY COUNCIL . . . 98

IV. SUMMARY OF THE PRINCIPAL JUDGMENTS RELATING TO THE ORNAMENTS OF THE MINISTER AND THE CHURCH, 1845–1906 113

V. APPENDIX: THE CORONATION OF KING EDWARD VII. AND QUEEN ALEXANDRA 143

TABLE OF CASES CITED

	PAGE
ADAMS v. RUSH, 2 Stra. 1133	34
ASTLE v. THOMAS, 2 B. & C. 271	34
ATTORNEY-GENERAL v. PARKER, 3 Atk. 576	19
BAKER v. WOOD, 1 Curt. 507	25
BARDIN v. CALCOTT, 1 Hag. Con. 14	62
BATEMAN v. HOTCHKIN, 31 Beav. 486	40
BEAL v. LIDDELL, Moore's Special Report	114
BOYD v. PHILPOTTS, L. R. 4 A. & E. 297	123
BRADFORD v. FRY, 4 P. D. 93	128, 133, 135
BROCKMAN v. ALL OF ST. JOHN THE BAPTIST, WEST DERBY, Unreported	115, 138
CAWDREY'S CASE, 5 Co. 1	101
CLIFFORD v. WEEKS, 1 B. & A. 506	49
CLIFTON v. RIDSDALE, 1 P. D. 316	114, 124
COMBE v. EDWARDS, L. R. 4 A. & E. 390; 2 P. D. 354; 3 P. D. 103	124
COOPER v. BLAKISTON, [1907] 1 K. B. 336	47
COX'S CASE, 1 P. W. 32	112
DAVEY v. HINDE, [1901] P. 95; [1903] P. 221	114, 137, 138
DAVIS v. BLACK, 1 Q. B. 900	11
DAWSON v. WILKINSON, Ca. temp. H. 381	29
DE ROMÂNA v. ROBERTS, [1906] P. 332	17
DURST v. MASTERS, 1 P. D. 123, 373	127
EVANS v. ASCUITHE, W. Jones, 158; Palm. 457	88
ELPHINSTONE v. PURCHAS, L. R. 3 A. & E. 66	118, 131, 133
Ex parte BLACKMORE, 1 B. & Ad. 122	16
Ex parte DALE, 6 Q. B. D. 376	124
Ex parte ENRAGHT, 6 Q. B. D. 376	124
Ex parte READ, 13 P. D. 221	130
FAULKNER v. LITCHFIELD, 1 Rob. E. 184	114
FLAMANK v. SIMPSON, L. R. 2 A. & E. 116	115
FORD v. CHAUNCEY, 1 Hag. Con. 382 (n)	28
FREELAND v. NEALE, 1 Rob. E. 643	51
FRYER v. JOHNSON, 2 Wils. 28	16
GILBERT v. BUZZARD, 3 Phillim. 349	16
GORHAM v. BISHOP OF EXETER, 15 Q. B. 52	87 (n)
GREENSLADE v. DARBY, L. R. 3 Q. B. 421	43
HAKES v. COX, [1892] P. 110	126
HALL v. ELLIS, Noy, 133	49
HARRISON v. BURWELL, Vaugh. 206	14
HEBBERT v. PURCHAS, L. R. 3 P. C. 605	121, 123, 131, 132
HOARE v. OSBORNE, L. R. 1 Eq. 585	60
HODGSON v. DILLON, 2 Curt. 388	51
HONYWOOD v. HONYWOOD, L. R. 18 Eq. 306	40
HOWELL v. HOLDROYD, [1897] P. 206	37
HUGHES v. EDWARDS, 2 P. D. 361	128, 136

xii TABLE OF CASES CITED

	PAGE
In re CHRIST CHURCH, EALING, [1906] P. 289	139
In re CHURCH OF ST. JOHN, ISLE OF DOGS, 4 T. L. R. 661; Tristram's Consistory Judgments, 67	129
In re HOLY TRINITY, HASTINGS, *Law Journal*, May 10th, May 17th, 1890	130
In re HOLY TRINITY, STROUD GREEN, 12 P. D. 199	129
In re ROBINSON, WRIGHT *v.* TUGWELL, [1892] 1 Ch. 95; [1897] 1 Ch. 85	121, 133
In re ST. AGNES, TOXTETH PARK, 11 P. D. 1	129
In re ST. ANSELM, PINNER, [1901] P. 202	136
In re ST. AUGUSTINE'S, HAGGERSTONE, 4 P. D. 111; Tristram's Consistory Judgments, 60	128
In re ST. GEORGES, JESMOND, *Law Journal*, June 22, 1889; *Guardian*, June 5, 1889	129
In re ST. LAWRENCE, PITTINGTON, 5 P. D. 131	128
In re ST. MARK'S, MARYLEBONE ROAD, [1898] P. 114	114, 135
In re ST. MARY'S, CHESTER, *Times* of June 15th, 1906; *Guardian* of June 20th and August 8th, 1906	115, 140
In re ST. PAUL'S, WILTON PLACE, Tristram's Consistory Judgments, 120	129
In re SARGENT, 15 P. D. 168	17
In re TYLER, [1891] 3 Ch. 252	60
KEMP *v.* ATTENBOROUGH, 30 L. T. 211; 25 J. P. 627	56
KEMP *v.* WICKES, 3 Phillim. 276	4
KENSIT *v.* RECTOR, etc., of ST. ETHELBURGA, BISHOPSGATE WITHIN, [1900] P. 80	114, 136
LAWRENCE *v.* JENKINS, L. R. 8 Q. B. 274; 42 L. J., Q. B. 147	38
LAWRENCE *v.* JONES, Bunb. 173	44
LEMAN *v.* GOULTY, 3 T. R. 3	34
LIDDELL *v.* BEAL, Moore's Special Report	115
LIDDELL *v.* WESTERTON, Moore's Special Report	115
LUCY *v.* BISHOP OF ST. DAVID'S, 1 Ld. Raym. 447; 12 Mod. Rep. 237; Carth. 484	82
MAIDMAN *v.* MALPAS, 1 Hag. Con. 205	61
MARKHAM *v.* VICAR, etc., OF SHIREBROOK, [1906] P. 239	115, 139
MARTIN *v.* MACKONOCHIE (first suit), L. R. 2 A. & E. 116; L. R. 2 P. C. 365	115, 116, 117, 119, 123
MARTIN *v.* MACKONOCHIE (second suit), L. R. 4 A. & E. 279	122
MASTIN *v.* ESCOTT, 2 Curt. 700; 4 Moo. P. C. C. 104	4
MATTHEW *v.* BURDETT, 2 Salk. 412	111
MIDDLETON *v.* CROFT, 2 Stra. 1056; 2 Atk. 640	92, 112
MILLAR *v.* PALMER, 1 Curt. 540	30
NAYLOR *v.* SCOTT, 2 Ld. Raym. 1558	19
NEVILL *v.* BRIDGER, L. R. 9 Ex. 214	20
NORTH MANCHESTER OVERSEERS *v.* WINSTANLEY, [1907] 1 K. B. 27; W. N. November 10th, 1906	42
NORTHWAITE *v.* BENNETT, 2 C. & M. 316	31
O'BRIAN *v.* KNIVAN, Cro. Jac. 552	68
PARKER *v.* CLERK, 3 Salk. 87; 6 Mod. Rep. 252	56
PATTEN *v.* CASTLEMAN, 1 Lee, 387	18
PHILPOTTS *v.* BOYD, L. R. 6 P. C. 435	123, 136
PIRBRIGHT *v.* SALWEY, W. N. 1896, 86	60
POOLE *v.* BISHOP OF LONDON, 7 Jur. N. S. 347	55
POPPLEWELL *v.* HATFIELD, 2 Wood, 398	45
RAND *v.* GREEN, 6 Jur. N. S. 303	32
READ *v.* BISHOP OF LINCOLN, 14 P. D. 88, 148; [1891] P. 9; [1892] A. C. 644; Roscoe's Report	82, 130, 131
RECTOR, ETC., OF ST. ANDREW'S, ROMFORD, *v.* ALL HAVING INTEREST, [1894] P. 220	133
RECTOR, ETC., OF BARSHAM *v.* PARISHIONERS OF SAME, [1896] P. 256	134
RECTOR, ETC., OF ST. LUKE'S, CHELSEA, *v.* WHEELER, [1904] P. 257	138

TABLE OF CASES CITED xiii

	PAGE
RECTOR, ETC., OF ST. STEPHEN, WALBROOK, v. SUN FIRE OFFICE, Tristram's Consistory Judgments, 103	43
REG. v. ARCHBISHOP OF CANTERBURY, 11 Q. B. 483; Jebb's Hampden Case	65 (n)
REG. v. BENSON, Phillimore's Eccl. Law. Vol. I. pp. 588, 589	8
REG. v. BISHOP OF LONDON, 23 Q. B. D. 414; 24 Q. B. D. 213	123
REG. v. HALL, 35 L. J., M. C. 251; 1 L. R., Q. B. 632	46
REG. v. HARDING, 6 T. L. R. 53	27
REG. v. MOORHOUSE-JAMES, 4 Cox C. C. 217	11
REG. v. O'NEILL, 31 J. P. 742	36
REG. v. SPURRELL, 1 L. R., Q. B. 72	26
REX v. ARCHBISHOP OF CANTERBURY, [1902] 2 K. B. 503	64, 88
REX v. ARCHBISHOP OF YORK, 6 T. R. 490	112
REX v. COLERIDGE, 2 B. & A. 808	16
REX v. MASHITER, 6 Ad. & E. 153	19
RICH v. BUSHNELL, 4 Hag. Ec. 164	62
RICKARD v. ROBSON, 31 Beav. 244	60
RIDSDALE v. CLIFTON, 2 P. D. 276	87, 122, 124, 125, 126, 127, 131, 132, 135, 136
RUGG v. KINGSMILL, L. R. 2 P. C. 59	63
SAUNDERSON v. CLAGGETT, 1 P. W. 656; 1 Stra. 420	47
SHEPHARD v. PAYNE, 12 C. B., N. S. 414; 16 C. B., N. S. 132; 31 L. J., C. P. 297; 33 L. J., C. P. 158	48
SOWERBY v. FRYER, L. R. 8 Eq. 417	41
SPRY v. GUARDIANS OF MARYLEBONE, 2 Curt. 5	15
STILEMAN-GIBBARD v. WILKINSON, [1897] 1 Q. B. 749; 13 T. L. R. 145	49
STOUGHTON v. REYNOLDS, 2 Stra. 1044; Ca. temp. H. 274	21, 35
STRACHY v. FRANCIS, 2 Atk. 217	39, 41
SUMNER v. WIX, L. R. 3 A. & E. 58	118, 119
TOPSALL v. FERRARS, Hob. 175	18
VELEY v. PERTWEE, L. R. 5 Q. B. 573	31, 36, 48
VICAR, ETC., OF GREAT BARDFIELD v. ALL HAVING INTEREST, [1897] P. 185	135
VICAR, ETC., OF PAIGNTON, v. ALL HAVING INTEREST, [1905] P. 111	138
VICAR OF THE PARISH OF THE ANNUNCIATION, CHISLEHURST, v. PARISHIONERS OF SAME, 4 P. D. 114; Tristram's Consistory Judgments, 67	128
VICAR OF RICHMOND, ETC., v. ALL HAVING INTEREST, [1897] P. 70	135
VICAR OF ST. JAMES, NORLAND, v. PARISHIONERS OF SAME, [1894] P. 256	133
VICAR OF ST. JOHN, PENDLEBURY, v. PARISHIONERS OF SAME, [1895] P. 178	134
VICAR OF ST. JOHN THE BAPTIST, TIMBERHILL, v. RECTORS, ETC., OF SAME, [1895] P. 71	133
VICAR OF ST. PETER'S, EATON SQUARE, v. PARISHIONERS OF SAME, [1894] P. 350	133
WALTER v. MOUNTAGUE, 1 Curt. 253	43
WARDEN AND MINOR CANONS OF ST. PAUL'S v. DEAN OF ST. PAUL'S, E. & Y. Tithe Cases, 809; 4 Price, 65	58
WESTERTON v. LIDDELL, Moore's Special Report, 1 Jur. N. S. 1178	114, 123, 132
WHITE v. BOWRON, L. R. 4 A. & E. 207	122
WILLIAMS v. BROWN, 1 Curt. 53	51
WOODWARD v. PARISHIONERS OF FOLKESTONE, Tristram's Consistory Judgments, 177	128
WRIGHT v. ELDERTON, 1 Wood, 518	45
WRIGHT v. TUGWELL (In re Robinson), [1892] 1 Ch. 95; [1897] 1 Ch. 85	121, 133

POINTS OF CHURCH LAW

POINTS OF CHURCH LAW

Baptism.

Omissions in Baptismal Register.

A. B. asks for advice in the following peculiar circumstances:—

"A child was baptised two months after birth. The evidence not only of the parents but of the god-parents and the clerk is conclusive that the baptism took place in church nine years ago. There is no entry of his baptism in the registry of baptisms. Can this boy be conditionally baptised, when it is certain that he was baptised, or how can the omission be rectified?"

The case is one of considerable difficulty, on which it would be rash to assert a positive opinion. The law relating to the registration of baptisms is regulated by the statute 52 Geo. III., c. 146, section 3 of which enacts that in no case shall an entry of baptism be made by the officiating minister, unless prevented by sickness or other unavoidable impediment, later than within seven days after the ceremony of any such baptism shall have taken place. Penal consequences of a very stringent character are applied by sections 36 and 37 of 24 and 25 Vict., c. 98, to any person destroying, defacing, injuring, forging, or altering the register, or making any false entry therein, &c. It may be questioned whether interlineations inserted in good faith would come within the penalties of this statute; but no prudent person would venture to tamper with the register, even by way of remedying omissions, so long after the time allowed. Even were it permissible to insert an entry of the baptism at this distance of time, the entry must be signed by the person who performed the rite, who may be dead or removed to a distance.

The question of re-baptism is a very delicate point, fitter for a theologian to answer than a lawyer. A. B. speaks of the evidence of the parents, &c., as "conclusive" and the "certainty that the boy was baptised." But he forgets that, however "conclusive" to his mind and in common parlance the evidence may be, only a court of justice could pronounce it to be conclusive in law, and that the only legal evidence of baptism is precisely the entry in the register, which is missing. In law the child must be presumed not to have been baptised until satisfactory evidence of baptism, other than the entry in the register (since that does not exist), is produced before a competent tribunal. Probably this reasoning will fail to satisfy him that he would be justified in re-baptising. In any case the rubric as to conditional baptism at the end of the Office for the Private Baptism of Children appears not to apply to the case under consideration. That rubric contemplates only "such uncertain answers to the priest's questions as that it cannot appear that the child was baptised with water, in the Name of the Father, and of the Son, and of the Holy Ghost," &c.—in other words, it goes only to the form and matter, not to the fact of baptism.

If the point were one involving the right of succession to a title or to property, possibly the case might be met by an action to perpetuate testimony in the Court of Chancery. If the boy's friends are dissatisfied, and the matter is thought to be of sufficient importance, a statutory declaration of the fact of baptism, stating time, place, &c., attested by the parents, godparents, clerk, and the officiating clergyman, if he be still living, and deposited in the diocesan registry, would perhaps be the best way of overcoming the difficulty.

Error in Name at Baptism.

A question has been asked as to the proper course to be pursued when, through some accident or misapprehension, a child has been baptised by one name and registered in another.

By section 8 of the Registration of Births and Deaths Act, 1874, 37 and 38 Vict., c. 88, the parent or guardian of the child, or the minister or person who performed the rite of baptism, may, within twelve months next after the registration of the birth of the child, deliver a certificate containing the requisite alteration of name to the registrar, who shall forthwith, without any erasure, enter in the register-book the name mentioned in the certificate, which is then to be forwarded to the Registrar-General, together with a certified copy of the birth with the name so added. *Vide* Dale's *Clergyman's Legal Handbook*, seventh ed., p. 202. This provision applies only to the civil register of births, not to the baptismal register, which must not be altered upon any consideration whatever. But it sufficiently meets the case of a name rightly given at baptism, but wrongly entered in the baptismal register. The converse case of a name wrongly given at baptism through error or misapprehension on the part of the minister presents greater difficulty. The child cannot be re-baptised, and the parents would rightly refuse to be satisfied with the mere recognition of the desired name by the civil authorities. The old Canon Law power of the Bishop—believed to be still operative—to change the name at Confirmation could perhaps be invoked to set the matter right.

REGISTRATION OF BAPTISMS BY LAYWOMEN.

A correspondent inquires how a baptism performed on emergency by a laywoman should be registered, and whether her name, or that of the incumbent of the parish, should be entered.

The name of the woman, not that of the incumbent, should be inserted. In the statute 52 George III., c. 146, which regulates the registration of baptisms, &c., there is no reference to lay baptism, and it appears to be assumed throughout that the person "by whom the ceremony was performed," mentioned in Schedule (A) to the Act, will be the "rector, vicar, curate, or officiating minister," whose duty it is, under section 3, to record " every baptism, whether private or public." The whole question of lay baptism was exhaustively discussed in the Court of Arches by Sir John Nicholl in the case of *Kemp* v. *Wickes*, 3 Phillimore's *Reports*, p. 276 (1809); and again by Sir Herbert Jenner in *Mastin* v. *Escott*, 2 Curteis, p. 700 (1841); and by the Privy Council on appeal, 4 Moore's *Privy Council Cases*, p. 104. Those learned judges decided that lay baptism, though irregular, was not invalid (*fieri non debet, factum valet*), and that the express words of our present rubric, inserted in 1662, "minister of the parish (or, in his absence, any other lawful minister that can be procured)," must not be taken to override the ancient use of the Church, sanctioned both by Canon Law and the Common Law. Since the law recognises baptism by a laywoman, it seems to follow that her name would be rightly inserted in the register as the person " by whom the ceremony was performed."

The subject will be found very fully and learnedly discussed in Phillimore's *Ecclesiastical Law*, Vol. I., pp. 491–494, and in Stephens's *Laws Relating to the Clergy*, Vol. I., pp. 100–126.

Burial of Unbaptised Children.

Q. An incumbent inquires whether he can claim a fee for the burial of an unbaptised child either (1) when there is no service or (2) when there is a service at the grave-side authorised by the Bishop. It appears that parents sometimes neglect to take steps for the baptism of a dying infant in the hope that they will thereby escape funeral expenses and burial fees, as though the child had been still-born, and it is thought that the existence of a fee, if it could be lawfully demanded, would operate as a check on such negligence.

A. It would seem that no fee can be demanded in either case. Surplice fees are only payable where a service authorised by the Book of Common Prayer has been performed. The rubric prohibits the use of the Burial Service over unbaptised persons, and the service authorised by the Bishop being outside the Prayer-book and the Act of Uniformity altogether, no fee is due in respect of it. Possibly some fee for breaking the soil may be due by custom in the particular parish.

Marriage.

Banns of Marriage, Time of Publication.

A correspondent inquires what is the law as to the time of publishing banns of marriage and what possible consequences are involved in disobeying it.

The old rubric after the Nicene Creed in the Communion Service (never repealed, or altered by authority) ran as follows :—

"Then the curate shall declare unto the people what holy-days or fasting-days are in the week following to be observed. And then also (if occasion be) shall notice be given of the Communion ; *and the banns of matrimony published* ; and briefs, citations, and excommunications read," &c.

In consonance with which the rubric prefixed to the Marriage Service ran :—

"First the banns of all that are to be married together must be published in the church three several Sundays *or holy-days in the time of Divine Service immediately before the sentences for the Offertory*," &c.

In 1753 was passed Lord Hardwicke's Act "for the better preventing of clandestine marriages," 26 Geo. II., c. 33 (repealed by 4 Geo. IV., c. 76), section 1 of which enacted that :

"All banns of matrimony shall be published in an audible manner in the parish church . . . . according to the form of words prescribed by the rubric prefixed to the Office of Matrimony in the Book of Common Prayer, upon three Sundays preceding the solemnisation of marriage, during the time of Morning Service, or of Evening Service (if there be no Morning Service in such church or chapel upon any of those Sundays) immediately after the Second Lesson : . . . . and all other the rules prescribed by the said rubric concerning the publication of banns, and the solemnisation of matrimony, and not hereby altered, shall be duly observed."

[The punctuation is that followed in Vol. VII. of the *Statutes at Large*, ed. 1769, pp. 525-526.]

The difficulties that ensued will be found fully

discussed in Stephens's *Notes on the Book of Common Prayer*, Vol. II., pp. 1151-1154. The object of the statutory provision, according to that learned writer, was simply to provide for the publication of banns in remote country parishes where only an evening service was held. It was intended not to override, but to supplement the rubric, which equally had the force of statute law, and could only be *pro tanto* repealed, according to well-defined rules of law, in so far as its language was "plainly and necessarily inconsistent and irreconcilable with" the later statute :—

"But instead of acting upon these rules," he adds, "the clergy have construed the statute of Geo. II. as if it annulled the rubrics ; for they have chosen to make the words in the section 'after the Second Lesson' override the whole sentence, so as to apply to the Morning Service as well as to the Evening. Whereas if they had construed the Act and the rubrics *reddendo singula singulis* according to the rules of law," they should have continued to publish the banns at Morning Service after the Nicene Creed, as the rubric required.

The next step in the change was due to the unauthorised intervention of the printers. Bishop Phillpotts stated in the House of Lords in 1845 that the alteration in the rubrics by which they assumed their present form was made solely on the authority of the Curators of the Press at Oxford about the year 1809.—*Vide* Hansard's *Parliamentary Debates*, third series, Vol. LXXVIII., p. 22 ; Blunt's *Book of Church Law*, seventh edition, p. 128. With the view of bringing the rubrics into supposed conformity with the words of the statute, they obliterated the words italicised above in the rubric after the Nicene Creed, and changed the words italicised in the rubric prefixed to the Marriage Service, so as to make them run "during the time of Morning Service, or of Evening Service, (if there be no Morning Service,) immediately after the Second Lesson ; . . . ."

[The punctuation is that of an old Prayer-book of 1832.]

The provisions of the Act of Geo. II. as to publication of banns were reaffirmed in almost identical terms by section 2 of 4 Geo. IV., c. 76, the statute upon which our present law of marriage rests.

As to the effect of the change and the duty of the clergy in respect of it, there is a conflict of opinion. Bishop Horsley, in his primary Charge to the clergy of St. Asaph in 1806, went so far as to say that he thought it "very doubtful whether a publication after the Nicene Creed be, as the law now stands, any publication at all : and whether a marriage under such irregular publication be a good and valid marriage," and warned the clergy that, if they persisted in such irregularity, they would be guilty of a misdemeanour at Common Law, and liable to punishment. Dr. A. J. Stephens, writing about the year 1850, held strongly to the contrary opinion. Baron Alderson, in the case of *Reg.* v. *Benson*, in 1856, expressed the view that the statute had not altered the rubric.— *Vide* Phillimore's *Ecclesiastical Law*, Vol. I., pp. 588, 589. This view is adopted by the editors of Blunt's *Church Law* at p. 129. On the other hand, the editor of Dale's *Clergyman's Legal Handbook*, seventh edition, 1898, at p. 184, conceives it "to be clear that under this section and the present rubric the banns, whether at Morning or Evening Service, should be published after the Second Lesson." And in Hammick's *Marriage Law of England*, at p. 68, the same opinion is confidently asserted.

In the absence of any authoritative decision there appears to be little doubt that either practice may safely be followed. No court would be likely to declare a marriage invalid on the ground of irregular publication of banns, still less to visit the minister with penal consequences, in a case where either view of the law had been *bonâ fide* acted upon. The older usage of publication after the Nicene Creed has behind it the unrepealed rubric of 1662, while the more modern practice of publishing banns after the Second Lesson can shelter itself beneath a doubtful interpretation of the Georgian statutes, which has been acted upon for a great number of years. In neither case are any pains and penalties to be feared.

Residence for Banns of Marriage.

A correspondent puts the following questions with reference to the legal qualification as to residence necessary for the publication of banns :—

1. "If a stranger stays from Saturday to Monday each week with a friend in the parish, may his banns be published in the church of such parish?"

2. "If a stranger rents a room for a fortnight, and sleeps one night a week in it, is that sufficient residence to admit of the banns being published?"

The questions can best be answered by reference to the opinion of the late Sir Robert Phillimore, taken in 1861, and quoted in Hammick's *Marriage Law of England*, at p. 77. In reply to questions as to the meaning of the words "dwell," "residence," and "usual abode," used in the rubric, in Canon 62, in 4 Geo. IV., c. 76, and the other Marriage Acts, and as to the extent of the residence required, he wrote :—

"I am of opinion that the words referred to are satisfied by a lodging taken for fifteen days, in which the persons taking it occasionally sleep and reside. I do not think they are satisfied by the mere hiring of the lodgings without any residence therein. . . . I incline to think there must be a reasonable use of the lodgings. . . . I do not believe that the true intent of the law was to enforce more than fifteen days' *bonâ fide* residence in a parish in which the parties did not usually dwell."

There seems to be no doubt that merely staying with a friend in the manner suggested does not constitute a sufficient qualification for publication of banns, though in practice the law is frequently evaded in this manner. It may be doubted also whether sleeping one night a week in a hired room would come within Sir R. Phillimore's opinion as to a "reasonable" use of the room for the purposes of "residence." But in such a case, where the party acted *bonâ fide*, it may safely be assumed that no court would look too closely into the circumstances ; and in any case irregularity in the publication of banns does not invalidate a marriage subsequently solemnised. *Vide* Hammick on *Marriage*, p. 77, and section 26 of 4 Geo. IV., c. 76.

Sunday Weddings.

A correspondent asks whether a vicar has the right (1) to refuse to take weddings on Sunday, or (2) to demand extra fees for so doing.

The answer must be in the negative to both questions. The first point is discussed in Hammick's *Marriage Law of England*, 2nd ed., p. 215. After stating his opinion that "it is clear the incumbent is legally entitled to fix the hour at which he will marry parties" within the limits of the canonical hours for celebrating marriage, the author considers the probability of application being made to clergymen under the new law to marry couples on Sundays at the conclusion of the morning service, on the plea of saving the loss of a day's wages to the man or for other reasons :—

"It seems very questionable," he writes, "whether a clergyman would be justified in declining to celebrate these Sunday marriages on any ground of mere convenience, provided the parties tender themselves at the church after notice to him, and claim the performance of the service. At all events, it would hardly be prudent for him to refuse to marry them without the authority of the Bishop, or without consulting the Chancellor of the diocese."

Refusal to marry parties presenting themselves at a lawful time and after complying with the formalities required by law is an ecclesiastical offence, if not an indictable offence at Common Law. *Vide* Hammick on *Marriage*, p. 212 ; *Davis* v. *Black*, 1 Q. B., 900 (1841) ; *Reg.* v. *Moorhouse-James*, 4 Cox's *Criminal Cases*, 217 (1850).

It should be added that neither statute nor ecclesiastical law makes any distinction between Sundays and common days as to the celebration of marriages ; while the rubric as to receiving the Communion on the day of marriage in the First Prayer-book of Edward VI., though relaxed at the final revision of 1662, goes to show that the Church has rather encouraged than otherwise the solemnisation of matrimony on Sundays and holy-days.

(2) The amount of the fees payable depends on custom, which varies in different parishes. We never heard of a custom anywhere to pay double fees for marriages celebrated on Sunday, and such custom, if alleged, would require very strict proof.

TIME OF CELEBRATING MARRIAGE.

A question has been asked as to whether a clergyman is legally justified in beginning the marriage service when there is not time to complete it before three o'clock.

There is no precise point in the marriage ceremony at which the marriage can be said to be complete in law. Some would make it consist in the interchange of vows, the placing of the ring, the blessing by the priest, or all three. The old maxim *consensus facit matrimonium* points to the interchange of the marriage vows as the essence of the contract. Hammick, in his *Marriage Law of England*, says at p. 99 :—

"It has been held that a marriage celebrated outside the canonical hours would not, on that account, be invalid; and if the interchange or declaration of matrimonial consent, 'I, N., take thee, M., &c.,' be completed within the time limited, the non-completion of the rest of the office before the time expired would probably be of little importance."

By section 21 of 4 George IV., c. 76, any person solemnising matrimony at any other time than the canonical hours, except by special licence from the Archbishop of Canterbury, shall be deemed and judged to be guilty of felony and punished, upon conviction, by a long term of penal servitude. But any clergyman apprehensive of such serious consequences may rest assured that no court, if satisfied as to the *bona fides* of the person accused, would care to inquire too closely into the precise moment at which the marriage service was begun and ended.

Marriage between Cousins.

A correspondent observes that for over 1,500 years all marriages between cousins have been forbidden by the

Church, and asks whether there is any law or canon declaring such marriages to be legal.

The prohibition in Western Europe rested on a decree of the Fourth Council of Lateran, A.D. 1215, which reduced the prohibition from the seventh to the fourth degree, thereby, as the Canon Law accounted it, forbidding marriages between second cousins, or, according to the civilian mode of reckoning, between first cousins (*vide* Stephens on the *Laws Relating to the Clergy*, Vol. I., p. 712; *Catholic Dictionary*, s.v. "Consanguinity"; Hammick on the *Marriage Law of England*, p. 41). There has never been any express repeal of this prohibition by the Canon Law, but in England the prohibition has been constructively repealed by the statute law, which always prevails where the statute law and the Canon Law are at variance. Our present law of consanguinity rests upon the statute 32 Henry VIII., c. 38, which, repealed by Mary and revived in part by Elizabeth, is still in force, taken in conjunction with the Table of Kindred and Affinity put forth, it is said by his own authority alone, by Archbishop Parker in 1563, and Canon 99 of 1603, which enforced that Table. The statutes 25 Henry VIII., c. 22, "An Act for the establishment of the King's Succession," passed to validate the King's marriage with Queen Anne Boleyn; 28 Henry VIII., c. 7, "An Act for the establishment of the Succession of the Imperial Crown of this Realm," passed after that Queen's attainder; and 32 Henry VIII., c. 38, "Concerning pre-contract and degrees of consanguinity," enumerate the marriages which "by God's law" were prohibited, among which there is no mention of marriage between cousins. They were not so much positive enactments as prohibitions aimed at the dispensing power of Rome. The last-named statute concludes with the words, "And that no reservation or prohibition, God's law except, shall trouble or impeach any marriage without the Levitical degrees," which in the case of *Harrison* v. *Burwell*, Vaughan's *Reports*, p. 206 (1669), were construed to permit even the marriage of a man with the widow of his great-uncle as being "without the Levitical degrees." *Pari ratione* the marriage of cousins is legal. The subject will be found more fully discussed in the works already cited, and in Gibson's *Codex*, Vol. I., p. 408; Blackstone's *Commentaries*, Vol. I., p. 435, and Vol. II., p. 207; Burn's *Ecclesiastical Law*, Vol. II., p. 449; Stephens on the *Book of Common Prayer*, Vol. III., p. 1573; Geary on the *Law of Marriage and Family Relations*, pp. 7 and 31; and in Blunt's *Church Law* (seventh edition), pp. 138–144.

Burial.

BURIAL FEES.—INCUMBENT'S POWER OVER CHURCHYARD.

A correspondent inquires:—

1. Whether the fee paid to an incumbent at a funeral represents the value of the land taken for the grave or the consideration for his work in reading the service?

2. Whether an incumbent can legally appropriate land in the churchyard for the future use of a particular family—

(*a*) At the time of the burial of one member of it,

(*b*) Before any death in the family occurs,

(*c*) If the applicant is a non-parishioner?

1. Fees for burial in parish churchyards are not paid as the price of the land required for the grave, which the incumbent has no power to sell. Sir Simon Degge (*temp.* Charles II.) writes:—

"By the custom of England every person may be buried in the churchyard of the parish where he dies without paying anything for breaking the soil" (*Parson's Counsellor*, Part I., Chap. 12, ed. 1703, p. 175; ed. 1820, p. 216).

Cf. Brooke Little on the *Law of Burial*, third ed., 1902, p. 17 :—

"Every parishioner and inhabitant of a parish has a common law right to be buried in his parish churchyard or burial-ground."

But by custom in most parishes certain fees are payable to the incumbent for breaking the ground at an interment, and these form the larger proportion of the sums usually paid. There are, in addition, certain smaller fees, known as surplice fees, which, though originally forbidden by the Canon Law, are now by custom generally payable to the minister for performing certain offices of the Church (*vide* Phillimore's *Ecclesiastical Law*, Vol. II., p. 1250). The amount of such fees, except where regulated by lawful authority under statute, no less than the liability to pay them at all, depends upon custom and differs in different parishes.

Dr. Lushington, in *Spry* v. *Guardians of Marylebone*, 2 Curteis, at p. 10 (1839), defines "customary fees" as—

"Fees which have existed so long that the origin cannot be traced; it need not be shown that they commenced before the time of legal memory; it is sufficient to show that they have existed so far back as can be discovered."

Cripps's *Law of the Church and Clergy*, p. 662, says :—

"Originally all such customary fees seem to have been payable for the interment rather than for the performance of the burial service; but . . . . the question is not easy to be determined."

2. (*a* and *b*) An incumbent has no power to prejudice the rights of the parishioners in their common burial-ground, and the rights of his successor in the matter of

fees, by appropriating parts of the churchyard for the future use of particular families or individuals. Though the King's courts will by *mandamus* compel an incumbent to bury in the churchyard a corpse brought for burial in the usual and proper manner (*Rex* v. *Coleridge*, 2 Barnewall and Alderson's *Reports*, p. 808 (1819)), they will not compel him to bury it in a particular part of the churchyard—*vide* the remarks of Justices Bayley and Littledale in the case *Ex parte Blackmore*, 1 Barnewall and Adolphus' *Reports*, p. 122 (1830). An alleged custom for the inhabitants of a parish to bury their dead as near to their ancestors as possible was held to be bad in the case of *Fryer* v. *Johnson*, 2 Wilson's *Reports*, p. 28 (1755). The incumbent has an unfettered discretion as to the part of the churchyard in which he will permit burial.

As to exclusive rights of burial, *vide* Brooke Little on the *Law of Burial*, third edition, p. 20 :—

"The rector cannot lawfully grant away any part of the church or churchyard for the purpose of a vault for an individual or a family. . . . Nor has any parishioner an absolute right to have any portion of the churchyard set apart for his exclusive use."

And the remarks of Lord Stowell in *Gilbert* v. *Buzzard*, 3 Phillimore's *Reports* (1820), at p. 357 :—

"The legal doctrine certainly is that the common cemetery is not *res unius aetatis*, the exclusive property of one generation now departed; but is likewise the common property of the living, and of generations yet unborn, and subject only to temporary appropriation. There exists a right of succession in the whole, a right which can only be lawfully obstructed in a portion of it, by public authority, that of the Ecclesiastical Magistrate [*i.e.*, the Ordinary] who gives occasionally an exclusive title in a part of the public cemetery to the succession of a single family, or to an individual who has a claim to such a distinction, but he does not do that without just consideration of its expediency, and a due attention to the objections of those who oppose such an alienation from the common use. Even a brick grave without such an authority is an aggression upon the common freehold interest, and carries the pretensions of the dead to an extent that violates the just rights of the living."

There is but one means whereby exclusive rights of burial in perpetuity of the sort under consideration can be obtained, and that is by faculty from the Bishop's Consistory Court. Such rights have often been conferred in times past, both within and without the Church; but in these days a court would be slow to decree such a faculty, unless for some very special reason—*e.g.*, great munificence to the church of the parish. Incumbents have sometimes, without legal sanction, permitted parts of the churchyard to be railed off for the use of a particular family; but such grants are bad in law, and future incumbents would be justified in treating them as non-existent. To make the title good, a confirmatory faculty from the Ecclesiastical Court is necessary. (*c*) Such faculties have been granted, for good cause shown, to living non-parishioners, in *In Re Sargent*, 15 P. D. 168 (1890), and in *De Romána* v. *Roberts*, [1906] P. 332.

Rights of Burial in more Parishes than One. Fees to whom Payable.

A correspondent puts the following questions:—

(1) *Q*. Can any one claim rights of burial in more parishes than one? How does the matter stand with regard to a person dying in a strange parish while on

a visit, or in a hospital, or suddenly on the road as the result of an accident?

A. Every parishioner has the right to be buried in the burial-ground of his parish, and he does not lose this right by the fact of dying outside the parish. At Common Law every person has the right to be buried in the parish where he dies, and the parochial authorities cannot refuse to bury the body because the deceased was a non-parishioner. His representatives in the cases supposed would thus have a choice of burial-places. If a person is a duly qualified parishioner in more parishes than one, he would have rights of burial in all.

The law on the subject as stated by Mr. Brooke Little in the *Law of Burial*, 3rd ed., 1902, at p. 17 (and in Degge's *Parson's Counsellor*), will be found quoted above at pp. 14, 15.

And in Cripps's *Law of the Church and Clergy*, p. 646, the matter is thus succinctly referred to:—

"The Canon Law principle was *ubi decimas persolvebat vivus, sepeliatur mortuus*. A stranger and foreigner therefore would, according to that law, have had no absolute right to burial in the parish where he died, except such right as arises out of necessity. . . . . It appears that a parishioner dying out of his parish has a right to be buried where he dies; or, if his relatives wish to remove him, that he has also a right to be buried in the churchyard of his own parish, *ubi decimas persolvebat vivus*."

(2) *Q.* Should a fee be paid to the minister of the parish where a person dies, though the burial be in another parish?

A. The point was decided in the negative in the King's Bench in the case of *Topsall* v. *Ferrars*, Hobart's *Reports*, p. 175 (1618); and in the case of *Patten* v. *Castleman*, 1 Lee's *Reports*, p. 387 (1753), the general principle was affirmed by Sir Geo. Lee, Dean of the Arches, that " where no service is done, no fee can be due." This latter case is adverse also to the claim that a fee can be due to the incumbent of a parish of which the deceased was a parishioner, though the body was buried elsewhere. *Cf.* Brooke Little, *Law of Burial*, 3rd ed., p. 43; the case of *Naylor* v. *Scott*, 2 Lord Raymond's *Reports*, p. 1558 (1729), in which it was held that an alleged custom to pay fees where no service had been rendered was void.

BURIAL OF NON-PARISHIONERS.

With reference to a case in which a clergyman demanded double fees for burying a non-parishioner *who died within the parish* while visiting a relative, questions were asked as to " Who is a parishioner ? " and under what circumstances double fees for burial can be claimed.

Section 32 of the Burial Act, 1852, 15 and 16 Vict., c. 85, associates the word " parishioners " with the words " inhabitants of the parish," and section 8 of 20 and 21 Vict., c. 35, an Act relating to interments in the Metropolis, defines the words " parishioner " or " inhabitant " as " a person inhabiting a house or dying in one of the parishes in the city of London or the liberties thereof." In the cases of *Attorney-General* v. *Parker*, 3 Atkyns's *Reports*, p. 576 (1747), and *Rex* v. *Mashiter*, 6 Adolphus and Ellis, p. 153 (1837), a very wide meaning is given to the word " inhabitant."

" It is now the common law of the country that every person may at this day be buried in the churchyard of the parish where he dies."—Cripps, *Law of the Church and Clergy*, p. 645.

" If the broad statement of Degge [quoted above, p. 14] is correct," writes Mr. Brooke Little in the *Law of Burial* (third edition), p. 162, "it would follow that not only 'parishioners' or 'inhabitants,' strictly so called, but also any person dying within the parish . . . . is entitled to be buried in the burial-ground [of such parish], and, if he has the right to be buried there, then the only fee legally payable is the fee charged for the burial of a 'parishioner,' and not of a 'non-parishioner,' as the fees chargeable for the burial of a non-parishioner may be so high as to be prohibitory, and therefore destructive of the right."

It is clear that in the case in question the clergyman had no right to demand double fees. He was bound to bury the body, and was only entitled to the fee commonly payable.

The right to charge burial fees for the burial of a non-parishioner *dying outside the parish* on a higher scale than the customary fees is recognised in *Nevill* v. *Bridger*, L.R. 9 Ex. 214 (1874).

Vestries.

Vestry Meetings.

The minister is *ex officio* chairman of the meeting, but cannot nominate a deputy. In his absence the parishioners elect a chairman, who must be an inhabitant of the parish.—Shaw's *Parish Law*, 7th ed., 1892, p. 560; Prideaux's *Churchwardens' Guide*, 16th ed., 1895, p. 138; 58 Geo. III., c. 69, s. 2.

All persons assessed and rated for the relief of the poor, whether resident in the parish or not, are entitled to attend and vote.—58 Geo. III., c. 69, s. 2, and 59 Geo. III., c. 85, s. 1. Women, if they possess the requisite qualifications as ratepayers, may vote. With regard to persons under age there appears to be no express authority on the point; but the presumption, regard being had to the disabilities under which the law places them in other respects, is against their being entitled to vote.

VICAR'S RIGHT TO VOTE AT VESTRY MEETINGS.

A correspondent inquires whether a newly appointed vicar, whose name had not been entered on the rate-book, was entitled to vote and give a casting vote at the Easter Vestry.

The vicar was clearly entitled to vote : s. 4 of *Sturges Bourne's* Act, 58 Geo. III., c. 69, enacts :—

"That when any person shall have become an inhabitant of any parish, or become liable to be rated therein, since the making of the last rate for the relief of the poor thereof, he shall be entitled to vote for and in respect of the lands, tenements, and property for which he shall have become liable to be rated, and shall consent to be rated, in like manner as if he should have been actually rated for the same."

Independently of the statute, it would seem that the vicar has at Common Law the right of voting in respect of his freehold. *Vide* the judgment of Lee, J., in *Stoughton* v. *Reynolds* (1736), *Cases temp. Hardwicke*, at p. 277 :—

"There is no difference as to the precedency of the parson in voting above the rest of the parishioners, only this distinction, that the parishioners vote in respect of their assessments, the parson votes in respect of his freehold, and, therefore, it has been said he may vote, though he pays no assessments."

As to the casting vote, *vide* Wills's *Vestryman's Guide*, p. 32 :—

"To this privilege he is entitled by universal custom;

but it is also specially confirmed to him by *Sturges Bourne's* Act, section 2."

Procedure at Vestry Meetings.

A correspondent asks for advice as to the legal duties of a vestry meeting, and what matters the chairman would be justified in ruling out of order for discussion.

Though the powers of vestries have been greatly curtailed since the passing of the Local Government Act, 1894, 56 and 57 Vict., c. 73, it would still hardly be possible to give an exhaustive list of all the matters which might properly come before them. Generally speaking, the functions of a vestry are now confined to such matters as the election of churchwardens, passing the churchwardens' accounts, sanctioning applications for faculties to make alterations in the fabric of the church, &c. The discussion of items in the parish accounts opens up a wide field of topics, and a prudent chairman will allow considerable latitude to parishioners who may desire to avail themselves of what is practically their only opportunity to state objections and air grievances in their only constitutional assembly. It is impossible to lay down any hard-and-fast rule as to what matters the parishioners may legitimately discuss, and the powers of the chairman in repressing or limiting discussion. The vestry has no voice in the appropriation of money taken at the offertory, and any attempt to raise the question would rightly be ruled out of order. But in such matters as the method of performing Divine service, or the choice of a site for a parish room, in which, though in strictness outside their province to determine, the parishioners are interested, reasonable opportunities for discussion should be afforded.

Some useful remarks of Sir Alfred Wills (*Vestryman's Guide*, 1855, p. 29) are worth quoting :—

"The powers and duties of the chairman, whether he be minister or parishioner, are similar to those of a chairman at any other meeting for the despatch of business, and are regulated by custom rather than by enactment or by positive law. His duty is to see that the business for which the meeting is called is brought before the vestry in due and proper form, that all legal requisites are attended to, that all persons who wish it may address the meeting, and that the sense of the meeting is fairly taken on any propositions or resolutions upon which it may have to decide. For these purposes, he is armed with a considerable amount of general authority, to maintain regularity and decorum, to repress extraneous discussion, and to give persons desirous of so doing opportunities of proposing resolutions not irrelevant to the business of the meeting."

Cf. Rogers on *Ecclesiastical Law*, ed. 1849, *sub voce* "Vestry," p. 955 :—

"Whilst the business is actually in progress, he may, and he ought, adopting the well-established rules of public meetings, to regulate, control, and direct the course and order of proceedings, and in cases of difference of opinion, so to order and conduct his arrangements as to enable every member to express his opinion, and, if necessary, give his vote without personal inconvenience or difficulty, whereby the real opinions of the voters may be ascertained in a satisfactory and impartial manner."

Polls at Vestry Meetings.

"Querist" asks for information as to (1) whether the chairman of a vestry meeting, at which a poll is demanded on behalf of a candidate for the office of churchwarden, is bound to grant a poll only " provided the candidate will give a written guarantee of the expenses of such poll." (2) What would be the *necessary* expenses if the chairman—*i.e.*, the vicar—declines to preside at this poll. (3) When and by whom the hours of polling are to be fixed.

1. The question is one of considerable difficulty. The chairman is bound to grant a poll if on a show of hands it be legally demanded by any person duly qualified to vote, and the fact that no guarantee for the expenses of the poll was forthcoming would be no valid ground for refusal. At the same time it seems very doubtful whether he is bound to incur any personal expense in the matter. The point will be found discussed in Shaw's *Parish Law*, 7th ed., 1892, " Note as to the expenses of the poll at the vestry," Appendix V., p. 607, as follows :—

" A question that naturally arises is—If the person demanding a poll at the vestry is not liable for expenses, and the chairman is bound to take the poll, how is the chairman to recover his expenses? Curiously enough there is very little authority on the point. None of the text-books, either on parish or ecclesiastical law, appear to give any information on the subject ; but we believe that the general opinion of lawyers is that the chairman has, as a general rule, no legal right to recover the expenses out of the rates."

" If this view is correct," he adds, " and the chairman is obliged to pay the cost of the poll out of his own pocket, his position is certainly a very hard one. For he is bound to take the poll, and to take it so that a fair opportunity is given to the ratepayers to record their votes. . . . The absence of direct authority is not very extraordinary. In most parishes polls are extremely rare, and in small ones they can be taken without any expense. . . . On the whole, it is evident that no person should accept the honour of taking the chair at the vestry, unless he is willing to run a considerable risk of having personally to defray the expenses of any poll that may be taken."

It would seem that the chairman will have done his duty if he gives notice, on a poll being demanded, that he will be ready, in person or by deputy, to take the votes of the ratepayers at such a time and place, but that he is not bound in a populous parish to give orders for taking the poll in a manner entailing great expense. The vicar can, of course, escape all liability, if he pleases, by simply absenting himself from the meeting, in which case the ratepayers present would elect a chairman from among themselves.

2. The question is not very clearly stated. Presumably the expenses would be for such matters as giving notice to the proper persons to produce the rate-books, precautions for maintaining order at the poll, and the like. Printing and the erection of polling-stations could hardly be said to come under the head of " necessary " expenses.

3. It is usual for the chairman to give notice of the time and place of holding the poll at the time when the poll is demanded, but the arrangements could be varied, if necessary, by subsequent notice. The poll should be kept open a sufficient time to allow all the parishioners who choose to come to be able conveniently to do so. *Vide* Shaw's *Parish Law*, 7th ed., 1892, p. 566; *Baker* v. *Wood*, 1 Curteis, p. 507 (1834). "The chairman," says Sir Alfred Wills, *Vestryman's Guide* (1855), at p. 50, " ought always, in fixing the time and place of the poll, to state at what hour it will be closed."

Churchwardens.

Who May be Churchwardens.

(1) A correspondent inquires whether a bank manager, who occupies the upper floors of the bank premises, the property of the company, free of rent, rates, and taxes, is eligible for the office of churchwarden.

The question is one of some difficulty in the absence of any direct legal decision on the point. The old cases and text-writers for the most part approach the subject from the point of view of the liability to serve an office from which every one was anxious to escape. The question was not so much who was eligible for, but who could be compelled to serve the office. Modern legislation having relieved churchwardens of the more onerous functions which they formerly discharged, the point of view has shifted, and the earlier *dicta* have to be considered in the light of eligibility rather than of liability to serve, which are not quite the same thing. The authorities are at one in saying that a churchwarden must be a resident inhabitant of the parish, and that he ought to be a householder. *Vide* Prideaux, *Churchwardens' Guide*, 16th ed., pp. 6 and 9; Shaw's *Parish Law*, 7th ed., 1892, p. 45; and Sir Lewis Dibdin's *Memorandum on the Election of Churchwardens, for the Use of the Diocese of Rochester* (1893), p. 17. Furthermore, it would seem that he must be also a ratepayer, since otherwise he would have no right of attending the meetings of the vestry. *Vide* Sir Alfred Wills's *Vestryman's Guide* (1855), p. 3. Formerly churchwardens were *ex officio* overseers of the poor by the statute 43 Eliz., c. 2, and it was held in the case of *Reg. v. Spurrell*, 1 L. R. Q. B. 72 (1865), that a servant who occupies a house of his master in part payment of his services, and as subservient thereto and necessary for the performance thereof, is not a "substantial householder" within the meaning of that statute. But the two offices no longer go together, and the term "householder" would, in all probability, be construed less strictly when applied to the office of churchwarden, which is a common-law office not resting on statute. For all practical purposes "householder" may be taken in this connexion to mean a person who has a home or hearth in the parish. In the case of *Reg.* v. *Harding*, 6 *Times* Law Reports, at p. 54 (1889), Lord Coleridge laid it down that for a man to be a churchwarden "it was necessary that he should live in the parish, be acquainted with the parishioners, and thus able to exercise the duties of his office, which were to be personally exercised." In the case of a doubtful election the issue can always be raised in a court of law on either side by applying for a *mandamus* to the Archdeacon, if he refuse to admit the churchwarden-elect, or to the parishioners to elect a new churchwarden, if the election is disputed. In the case submitted there seems no reason to suppose that the candidate would be held by the court to be ineligible.

(2) "Deaconess," who rents from her husband, the vicar, a cottage situate on and belonging to the vicarage grounds, inquires whether she is thereby qualified as a householder in the parish and rendered eligible for election as churchwarden.

To be eligible for the post of churchwarden a person must be a resident inhabitant—*i.e.*, "a householder in the parish, personally occupying a house in the parish, though not, perhaps, necessarily resident therein." Mere occupation of lands or payment of rates without residence will not suffice (Prideaux, *Churchwardens' Guide*, ed. 1895, pp. 6–9).

"An inhabitant, to be qualified for the office of churchwarden, must in some sense be a resident in the parish. . . . By the word *householder* is meant a person who occupies as tenant" (Steer's *Parish Law*, 6th ed., 1899, p. 105; Shaw's *Parish Law*, 7th ed., 1892, p. 45).

In the case under consideration it would seem that the lady's occupation of the premises is sufficient to bring her within these limitations, and that she is legally qualified for the post of churchwarden if she desires to be elected. Women are, of course, sometimes admitted churchwardens, though their right to be so has been questioned.

Lodgers as Churchwardens.

Q. A correspondent mentions the case of a lodger, who being neither a householder nor a ratepayer, though resident in the parish, has been nominated by the rector as his warden and admitted by the Archdeacon at his Visitation in spite of a protest. He asks whether the appointment was valid, and, if not, how the man can be deprived of office.

A. "A mere lodger or inmate is not qualified for the office of churchwarden."—*Vide* Prideaux, *Churchwardens' Guide* (16th edition), p. 9, citing *Ford* v. *Chauncey*, Haggard's *Consistory Reports*, I., p. 382 (n), (1715). "Occupation of a house is necessary; and hence a mere lodger is not liable to serve" (Shaw's *Parish Law*, 7th ed., 1892, p. 45). The only way to remove from office a person not duly qualified is by application to the High Court for a *mandamus* to compel the rector to nominate a fit and proper person.

LIABILITY OF CHURCHWARDENS.

A correspondent asks for information under the following circumstances :—

In November, 1899, the vicar's warden went to South Africa, leaving the people's warden in sole charge of the parish as churchwarden. A small customary payment for insuring the church was made by the people's warden at Christmas, the clerk's salary being left unpaid. The accounts, showing a small deficit, were duly passed at the Easter Vestry meeting. Differences of opinion, on the return of the vicar's warden, having arisen as to the liability of the latter for disbursements made in his absence without his sanction and knowledge, and as to the propriety of some of the payments, the following questions have been submitted :—

1. Who is legally liable to pay the deficit?

2. Can the vicar's warden repudiate all liability for the sum paid for insurance?

1. The case is one of considerable difficulty, the questions of the liability of churchwardens for debts incurred in the discharge of their office and the means of calling them to account being somewhat obscure.

Formerly expenditure required for church purposes was covered by a rate. The churchwardens called a meeting of the vestry, submitted an estimate of the sums necessary, and received authority from the vestry to levy a rate upon the whole parish for the amount. If the rate and the expenditure did not balance one another, the churchwardens were not merely not required to find the money out of their own pockets, but it was even considered illegal for them to do so. Thus, in *Dawson* v. *Wilkinson*,

Cases King's Bench, *temp.* Hardwicke, p. 381 (1737), Justice Chapple said :—

"It is very plain . . . . that there cannot be a rate made to reimburse the churchwardens, because they are not obliged to lay any money out of their own pockets."

And in *Millar* v. *Palmer*, 1 Curteis, at p. 547 (1837)— a case in which criminal proceedings were taken against churchwardens for neglecting to repair a church—Dr. Lushington, then Chancellor of the diocese of London, went so far as to declare :—

"Nothing is more clear than that they are not bound, and that it is illegal in them to expend their own money, or incur debt."

And Sir H. Jenner-Fust on appeal to the Court of Arches said : "The churchwardens were not bound to expend their own money, nor to undertake the repairs until the funds were provided" (*ibid.* 555).

But the Compulsory Church Rate Abolition Act, 1868, 31 and 32 Vict., c. 109, by taking away the power to enforce church rates by legal process, rendered much of the law on the subject obsolete, and introduced uncertainty and confusion into questions affecting parochial finance. In the days of compulsory church rates, if there was a deficit in the parish accounts, it was the duty of the churchwardens to summon a meeting of the vestry and obtain authority to levy a fresh rate. In spite of the alteration in the law, this method, though unpopular and little used now, is still the proper legal means of making good a deficit. The vestry should be asked to authorise the raising of a voluntary rate, refusal to pay which disqualifies the person so refusing from "inquiring into, objecting to, or voting in respect of the expenditure of the moneys arising" therefrom by virtue of section 8 of the Act already mentioned.

In practice, however, church expenses are now usually met by voluntary contributions, not in the nature of a rate, for the custody and due appropriation of which churchwardens are accountable to the parish, and in the last resort to the Ordinary. Though, as it would seem, they are not personally liable to the vestry or to their successors for any deficit in their accounts at the close of their year of office, they are personally liable, jointly or severally as the case may be, by way of contract, to any person—*e.g.*, a carpenter, or gas-fitter—who has done work in or about the church or church-yard by their order (*vide* Shaw's *Parish Law*, 7th ed., 1892, p. 58 ; Prideaux's *Churchwardens' Guide*, 16th ed., 1895, p. 109, and the cases there cited). But one church-warden cannot pledge the credit of his co-churchwarden without his knowledge (*Northwaite* v. *Bennett*, 2 Crompton and Meeson's *Reports Exchequer*, p. 316, 1834). In *Veley* v. *Pertwee*, L.R. 5 Q.B., p. 573 (1870), it was held that churchwardens were not liable to pay fees at the Visitation of an Archdeacon, if no funds available were in their hands.

In default of a rate, there is another way of dealing with a deficit, for which there is ample authority. The succeeding churchwardens may carry it over as an item in the parish accounts and account for it with other disbursements at the end of the year.

Wood, in his *Institute of the Laws of England*, ed. 1772, Book I., ch. 7, p. 92, writes :—

"If their receipts fall short of their disbursements, the succeeding churchwardens are bound to pay what is due to them, and account it amongst their disbursements to the parishioners at the end of the year."

Cf. Prideaux, *Directions to Churchwardens*, ed. 1730, p. 99 ; Rogers on *Ecclesiastical Law* (1849), p. 256.

On the general question of the liability of churchwardens to account, *vide* Meriton's *Guide for Constables, Churchwardens, &c.*, sixth ed. (1679), p. 156; Wood's *Institute, sup.*; Nelson's *Office and Authority of a Justice of Peace*, second ed. (1707), p. 141; Gibson's *Codex*, Vol. I., p. 166; Burn's *Ecclesiastical Law*, Vol. I., p. 413; Viner's *Abridgement* (1748), Vol. IV., p. 531.

2. The vicar's warden cannot justly take exception to the money paid for insurance. As he did not take the proper course of resigning his office on leaving the country, his absence from which would have been a sufficient ground for his removal by the Ordinary, and the election of a new churchwarden in his place, he must be held to have given an implied authority to his co-churchwarden to make all legal and necessary payments for the church on his behalf so far as there were funds in hand to meet them. That insurance is a proper and lawful subject of expenditure there appears to be no doubt. In the days of compulsory church rates church expenses were divided under two heads: *necessary*, for which the law required the vestry to make provision, and *allowable*, for which, though not required by law, the vestry could, if it pleased, make provision (*vide* Dale's *Clergyman's Legal Handbook*, seventh edition (1898), pp. 160, 161). In *Rand* v. *Green*, 6 Jur. N.S. p. 303 (1860), insurance was held to be one of these "allowable" items. If insurance is an item for which a rate could have been demanded in the old days, clearly it is a proper payment now. It is the duty of the incumbent under section 54 of the Ecclesiastical Dilapidations Act, 1871, to insure the chancel when he is liable to repair it. The text-books are silent as to the duty of the churchwardens to insure the body of the church. But the matter is a frequent subject of inquiry in Archdeacons' visitation articles and the like, and though in law churchwardens neglecting to

insure are not punishable in the ecclesiastical court, they would in these days justly be held censurable for neglecting so obvious a duty.

At the same time, the old distinction between " necessary " and " allowable " outgoings still holds good. The former should have priority over the latter, and, in strict law, a churchwarden who, with insufficient funds in his hands to meet both, applied the money to an " allowable " purpose, however suitable, to the exclusion of " necessary " payments, might be held to have done so at his own risk. The sum due to the clerk for salary appears to come under the head of " necessary " payments. Clerks, according to Canon 91—

"Shall have and receive their ancient wages, without fraud or diminution, either at the hands of the churchwardens, at such times as hath been accustomed, or by their own collection, according to the most ancient custom of every parish."

The clerk's " ancient wages " are an item of expenditure known to the law, and should have had priority over even so important a matter as insurance.

It is exceedingly difficult to advise in a case of this kind, because the only method of procedure recognised by the law is one which the law itself has rendered obsolete. The only legal way of raising money for church expenses and supplying a deficit is by making a rate, which the law says should be levied, but will not enforce. In strictness, churchwardens are not justified in expending a single penny until they have approached the vestry and asked for authority to levy a rate. But the machinery for doing this no longer exists, and the whole system has become antiquated. The position of churchwardens, as regards both their duties and liabilities, requires to be reconsidered by the Legislature, and until such time as this can be done doubts and difficulties must of necessity arise.

In the case under consideration, if there is an objection to levying a rate, or to carrying the deficit over into the accounts for the current year, there would seem to be no impropriety, if the late churchwardens can adjust their differences, and the money cannot be raised in any other way—in spite of the *dictum* of Dr. Lushington quoted above, which applied to a very different state of the law—in dividing the balance, including the sum paid for insurance, equally between them, and making good the deficit, by way of private contribution, out of their own pockets.

REMEDIES AGAINST CHURCHWARDENS.

A churchwarden refusing to account to his successors for moneys which have passed through his hands can be " presented " to the Ordinary at his Visitation by the incoming churchwardens, and compelled to render an account by the spiritual court. But this court has no jurisdiction to inquire into the propriety of accounts so rendered.—*Adams* v. *Rush*, 2 Strange's *Reports*, p. 1133 (1740); *Leman* v. *Goulty*, 3 *Term Reports*, p. 3 (1789). It is asserted in most text-books, on the authority of a case heard in 1823, *Astle* v. *Thomas*, 2 Barnewall and Cresswell's *Reports*, p. 271, that an action lies at Common Law against a churchwarden refusing to account at the suit of the new churchwardens. *Cf.* Lambard's *Duties of Churchwardens* (ed. 1610), p. 72 :—

"The new officers may (by action of account) call to account the former churchwardens, and shall thereby compel them, both to give reckoning of their doings during their office, and also to make satisfaction to the use of the parish, for the harme that it hath received by their fault."

One modern text-writer expresses the opinion that "there appears to be no reason why churchwardens might not, like all other trustees, be called to account in Chancery by the proper parties."—Cripps's *Law of the Church and Clergy*, p. 194. The remedies against defaulting churchwardens are admittedly unsatisfactory.

Re-admission of Churchwardens continuing in Office and Payment of Fees.

Q. A correspondent mentions the case of a parish in which churchwardens, duly "admitted" when first appointed, took no steps at the ensuing Easter vestry to discharge themselves of their office, no fresh election being made, and inquires:—

(1) Do they continue in office?

(2) If continuing in office, do they need to be re-admitted as in the case of churchwardens who are re-elected?

(3) Are the fees claimed an annual charge on the office or offices, or are they only fees payable on formal admission to office?

A. (1) and (2) Churchwardens continue in office until their successors are appointed (*vide* Cripps, *Law of the Church and Clergy*, p. 181), and if re-elected should be re-admitted by the Archdeacon.—Prideaux's *Churchwardens' Guide*, 16th ed., 1895, p. 44; *Stoughton v. Reynolds*, 2 Strange's *Reports*, p. 1044 (1736). It is quite irregular for churchwardens to continue in office without re-election, and a vestry neglecting to elect could be compelled by *mandamus* from the High Court to proceed to an election In the case under consideration, the churchwardens undoubtedly continue in office with the same duties and liabilities as before. But they ought to be re-elected and re-admitted as soon as possible. (3) Their neglect to offer themselves for re-election does not exempt them from the duty of paying the customary fees. These fees are not fees on admission to office, as is commonly supposed, but fees payable in respect of the Archdeacon's Visitation, and all persons cited thereto ought to pay them. The fees were fixed by authority in 1869 in pursuance of the statute 30 and 31 Vict., c. 135. There is a widespread misconception among churchwardens up and down the country that they are not bound to pay the fees, because in a case decided shortly after the passing of that Act, and of the Compulsory Church Rate Abolition Act, 1868, *Veley* v. *Pertwee*, L. R. 5 Q. B., p. 573 (1870), it was held that where churchwardens have no money in their hands, and are without the means of obtaining funds, they are not liable to pay the fees out of their own pockets. But where they have funds in hand it is highly reprehensible (to say the least of it) to attempt to evade (as is too often the case) the obligation to pay fees which are due at Common Law and by the ecclesiastical law, and which have been expressly regulated by statute.

Custody and Distribution of Alms.

In the case of alms contributed at the offertory in the Communion Service the minister and churchwardens are jointly responsible for their distribution. If they disagree recourse must be had to the Ordinary—*vide* ninth post-Communion rubric. In the case of collections taken at other services the minister has a discretion as to the object to which the money shall be devoted. *Vide* remarks of Cockburn, C.J., in *Reg.* v. *O'Neill*, 31 J. P.

at p. 743 (1867),—a case in which the vicar had given notice that collections would be made for a particular object, and the people's warden had seized part of the money and retained it for another purpose :—

"It was not unlawful for the vicar to make such a collection, and having done so, he was in lawful possession of the money. The churchwarden had no right whatever to attempt to lay hold of the money to apply it to a different purpose."

As to the custody of alms collected, it was laid down by Dr. Tristram in *Howell* v. *Holdroyd*, [1897] P. p. 206, that "the churchwardens are the proper custodians of moneys collected for Church expenses." The same learned Chancellor expressed the opinion that in case of the—

"Refusal of one of the churchwardens to sign a joint cheque for the payment of Church expenses, the remedy is to article the churchwarden in the Ecclesiastical Court, and obtain an order admonishing him to sign the cheque, with condemnation in the costs of the suit."

Similarly, in the case of a churchwarden obstinately refusing to hand over money which he has collected in the ordinary course of his duty to be applied to an object approved by the vicar and his co-churchwarden, the remedy would seem to be by exhibiting articles against him in a criminal suit in the Consistory Court.

Churchyards.

Timber in Churchyards.

The vicar of L., of which the Dean and Chapter of H. are patrons, and presumably in receipt of the rectorial tithes, asks for advice under the following circumstances :—

In the churchyard are fourteen old elm-trees believed to be dangerous to the church and surrounding buildings. The space is limited, and the felling or polling which may be necessary would be attended by considerable risk. The parishioners object, on grounds of sentiment, to the removal of the trees. Graves are now being dug round one of the trees. The vicar desires to be informed—

1. Who would be liable for any damage to private property caused by the fall of the trees?

2. Who is entitled to the timber, or proceeds of the sale, if it falls, or in the event of the vicar deciding to fell the trees?

1. There is no decided case in which the owner of land has been held liable in damages for injury to property caused by trees falling by the "act of God"—*e.g.*, gale, landslip, flood, &c. But an owner of timber has been held responsible for damage caused by negligent felling or lopping (Addison on *Torts*, eighth ed. (1906), pp. 483, 484; *Lawrence* v. *Jenkins*, L. R. 8 Q. B., p. 274; 42 L. J. Q. B., p. 147 (1873)), and it is possible in the present case that the vicar might be held liable at Common Law for negligence, if it was proved that he knew of the dangerous state of the trees and took no steps to avert the danger, or that he knew that grave-digging near the roots of the trees was likely to imperil their safety. Similarly, in the case of monuments in the churchyard destroyed or injured by the fall of a tree, if negligence could be proved against the vicar, he would probably be held liable in damages to the executors or heirs of the deceased. The questions of fact and of the reasonableness of the vicar's exercise of his discretion would be points for the jury to determine in each case.

2. The vicar (or the rector impropriate) has the right to fell timber in the churchyard for the purpose of

repairing the chancel. *Vide* Gibson's *Codex*, Vol. I., p. 208 ; Watson's *Clergyman's Law*, ed. 1747, p. 388 ; Rogers on *Ecclesiastical Law*, p. 262 ; Cripps's *Law of the Church and Clergy*, p. 434. The law rests on the statue 35 Edward I., cap. 4, anno 1307, *Ne rector prosternat arbores in coemeterio*, as follows :—

" Forasmuch as a churchyard that is dedicated is the soil of a church, and whatsoever is planted belongeth to the soil, it must needs follow that those trees which be growing in the churchyard are to be reckoned amongst the goods of the church, the which lay-men have no authority to dispose : . . . .

" And yet seeing those trees be often planted to defend the force of the wind from hurting of the church ; We do prohibit the parsons of the church that they do not presume to fell them down unadvisedly, but when the chancel of the church doth want necessary reparations. Neither shall they be converted to any other use, except the body of the church doth need like repair ; in which case the parsons of their charity shall do well to relieve the parishioners with bestowing upon them the same trees, which we will not command it to be done, but we will commend it when it is done."

Lord Hardwicke, in the case of *Strachy* v. *Francis*, 2 Atkyns's *Reports*, p. 217 (1741), a motion by a patron to restrain the rector from committing waste by cutting down timber in the churchyard, laid it down that—

" A rector may cut down timber for the repairs of the parsonage-house, but not for any common purpose ; . . . . He may cut down timber likewise for repairing any old pews that belong to the rectory ; and he is also entitled to botes for repairing barns and outhouses belonging to the parsonage."

It will be seen that the rector or vicar has no right to

cut timber in the churchyard for his own benefit, and even in the case of timber severed from the soil by the "act of God," or as a necessary precaution for the safety of himself and the parishioners, his right to profit by the occurrence is by no means clear. The proper course in such a case would seem to be to carry the proceeds of the sale of any timber not required for the purpose of necessary repairs to an account for augmenting the value of the benefice. The position of an incumbent is analogous to that of the tenant for life of an estate impeachable for waste, who must do nothing to impair the inheritance. *Vide* the opinion of Sir J. Romilly, Master of the Rolls, in *Bateman* v. *Hotchkin,* 31 Beavan's *Reports,* p. 486 (1862) :—

"In the case of timber blown down by a storm, there is no waste, because it is the act of God, but the produce of the sale of it belongs to the inheritance, that is, the money must be invested in Consols, and the interest paid to the tenant for life." *Cf. Honywood* v. *Honywood,* L. R. 18 Equity, p. 306 (1874).

The incumbent in the present case would be entitled to the interest on the money invested during his tenure of the benefice.

The patron, as such, has no right whatever to the timber.

Lay Rector's Rights over Churchyard.

A country vicar feels himself aggrieved by the action of the lay rector of his church, who, without consulting the vicar, caused a quantity of ivy which had grown round the stems of some common fir-trees in the churchyard to be cut and left to die. The lay rector justifies his action on the ground that the destruction of the ivy was necessary to save the trees, which might at some future time be needed for the repair of the chancel. The vicar wishes to know what are the lay rector's rights in the churchyard as against the parishioners and himself.

It was long doubted, in cases where there is a rector and a vicar in the same church, to whom the trees in the churchyard belonged.—*Vide* Lyndwood's *Provinciale*, Oxford edition, 1679, p. 267. But it is now accepted, on the authority of Chief Justice Rolle, that they belong to him who is bound to repair; that is, in this case, the lay rector.—*Vide* Rolle's *Abridgement*, Vol. II., p. 337; Cripps's *Law of the Church and Clergy*, p. 435. But the rector, whether lay or spiritual, can only cut the trees for certain well-defined purposes connected with repairs, and if he cuts or lops in an arbitrary manner he can be restrained by an injunction in Chancery.—*Strachy* v. *Francis*, 2 Atkyns's *Reports*, p. 217 (1741). Trees cannot be cut down for the purpose of creating a general repairing fund. —*Sowerby* v. *Fryer*, L. R. 8 Equity, p. 417 (1869); Kerr on *Injunctions*, fourth edition (1903), pp. 63, 64. In the present case the lay rector appears to have acted within his rights.

The parishioners have no right to the timber even for repairing the body of the church, though in the quaint language of the statute (cited above, p. 39), *Ne rector prosternat arbores in coemeterio*, 35 Edward I., stat. 2, in such a case—

"The parsons of their charity shall do well to relieve the parishioners with bestowing upon them the same trees, which we will not command to be done, but will commend when it is done."

The Rating of Churchyards.

In the *Guardian* of July 25th, 1900, "Inquirer" raised a question as to whether churchyards are subject to local rate or not, to which a clerical correspondent replied that he had satisfied himself that churchyards *inter alia* are rated to the poor; but he gave no authority for the statement. The question was long in doubt, but appears to be now clear. At Common Law the churchyard appears to be one with the church, and the statute of 35 Edward I., *Ne rector prosternat arbores in coemeterio*, speaks of the churchyard as "the soil of a church."—*Vide supra*, p. 39. In the case of *North Manchester Overseers* v. *Winstanley*, [1907] 1 K. B., p. 27, and *Weekly Notes* of Nov. 10, 1906, it was held by Lord Alverstone, C.J., and Ridley and Darling, JJ., that a churchyard acquired under the Church Building Acts, in lieu of an old churchyard closed under Order in Council, was distinguishable from a cemetery maintained for purposes of private gain, was therefore not a rateable hereditament but a parish churchyard, and that, as such, it came within the exemptions of 3 and 4 Will. IV., c. 30, as a place "exclusively appropriated to public religious worship."

Care of Churchyards.

A question has been asked as to whether it is the duty of the vicar or the churchwardens to see that (1) the grass, (2) the paths of the churchyard are kept in order.

1. The freehold of the churchyard, subject to the use of the parishioners for all necessary purposes connected with Divine service and the burial of the dead, is in the incumbent, who has the right, generally speaking, to all profits arising therefrom; *e.g.*, the right to the herbage.—*Vide* remarks of Cockburn, C.J., in *Greenslade* v. *Darby*,

L. R. 3 Q. B. (1868), at p. 428, and of Dr. Tristram in *Rector and Churchwardens of St. Stephen, Walbrook,* v. *Sun Fire Office,* Tristram's *Consistory Judgments,* at p. 107 (1883). The vicar has the right to mow and remove the grass, but is under no obligation to do so, if he does not see fit.

It is the duty of the churchwardens to see that the churchyard is " well and sufficiently repaired, fenced, and maintained " in accordance with Canon 85. " They are the sole judges of what is needful to be done therein, as being invested with the authority of the Ordinary for that purpose " (Cripps, *Law of the Church and Clergy,* p. 435). It is their duty " to see that it be kept in a decent and fitting manner, that it be cleared of all rubbish, muck, thorns, briers, shrubs, and anything else that may annoy the parishioners when they come into it, or be any hindrance to them in the burying of their dead " (Prideaux's *Churchwardens' Guide,* 16th ed., 1895, p. 99). But it is less certain whether this duty extends to matters of neatness and ornament. Mere unsightliness may, perhaps, justify them in cutting and removing the grass; and if the untidy condition of the churchyard amounts to an obstruction, so as to prevent access to the church or interfere with the burial of the dead, their duty is clear. But to cut and remove the grass merely to improve the appearance of the churchyard contrary to the wishes of the vicar might lay the churchwardens open to an action for trespass. In the absence of positive authority on the point the case seems one that can only be satisfactorily met by an arrangement between the vicar and churchwardens.

2. In the case of the churchyard footpaths the duty of the churchwardens admits of no doubt. Dr. Lushington, in *Walter* v. *Mountague,* 1 Curteis, at p. 260 (1836), lays it down that " the churchwardens by virtue of their office

are bound to see that the footpaths are kept in proper order and the fences in repair."

Easter Offerings and Visitation Fees.

Recovery of Easter Offerings.

A correspondent inquires whether Easter offerings are recoverable at law, and, if so, how much is due from each individual in the house.

The following remarks have reference only to those offerings which, like tithe, are of ancient origin, not to those voluntary gifts which are often in modern times made to the clergy at Easter by members of their congregations.

Easter offerings were at first part of the voluntary oblations of the people to the priest, which, becoming recognised by custom, came in time to be a matter of legal obligation.

Ayliffe, writing in 1726, says, " The offerings at Easter are due by custom; for they are not voluntary oblations, but are paid as a composition for personal tithes."— *Parergon*, p. 393.

Watson, *Clergyman's Law* (ed .1747), p. 585, speaks of:

" Those small accustomary sums commonly paid by every person when he receives the Sacrament of the Lord's Supper at Easter, which in many places is by custom two pence from every communicant, and in London a groat a house."

In the case of *Laurence* v. *Jones*, Bunbury's *Reports*, p. 173 (1724) :—

" It was decreed that Easter offerings were due of common right at 2*d.* per head, unless it had been customary to pay more. . . . . And it was said by Baron Gilbert that offerings were a compensation for personal tithes."

In *Wright* v. *Elderton*, 1 Wood, *Decrees in Tithe Causes*, p. 518 (1709), the vicar of Stepney was held to be entitled to 3*d.* yearly from each person in the parish above the age of sixteen in lieu of Easter offerings; and in *Popplewell* v. *Hatfield*, 2 Wood, *Decrees in Tithe Causes*, at p. 400 (1741), the Court of Exchequer made an order for the payment of 2*d.* for every inhabitant above the age of sixteen in respect of Easter offerings. It is unnecessary to enter into the controversy as to whether these offerings are due of common right or by custom. The latter is now the generally received opinion.

The right to receive accustomed offerings is recognised by the statute 2 and 3 Edward VI., c. 13, which is unrepealed as to " tithes, offerings and duties which have not been commuted, or are otherwise still payable."

" If there is no question about the custom, and that is clearly admitted," says Cripps, *Law of the Church and Clergy*, p. 351, " Easter offerings may be sued for, and ought to be sued for, in the spiritual court; but the spiritual court can have no power to determine the existence or non-existence of a custom. . . . . Whether Easter offerings could be recovered by a suit in a court of equity appears doubtful."

The matter, therefore, appears to stand thus :—A clergyman claiming to receive such offerings as of right would be put to the strictest proof of the particular local " custom," in the technical legal sense of the term, on which he based his claim. But, as the spiritual court cannot try a question of custom, a prohibition would issue from the King's Bench Division of the High Court, where the point of custom would have to be determined, before the spiritual court could deal further with the matter. If the Common Law court found that the custom existed, the offerings could then be sued for and recovered in the spiritual court. It will be seen that the recovery of Easter offerings by this process, though possible, would in these days be a matter of great difficulty. As to other modes of recovery, Sir Simon Degge (*Parson's Counsellor*, Part II., chap. 23, p. 345, ed. 1703, p. 422, ed. 1820) conceived that an action at Common Law could be founded on the statute of Edward VI., but the opinion has not been followed. Oblations (which would include Easter offerings) to the amount of £10 are recoverable in a summary manner before two Justices of the Peace under section 2 of 7 and 8 Will. III., c. 6, and section 4 of 53 George III., c 127, which are still operative for the purpose of recovering small uncommuted tithes and oblations.—*Reg.* v. *Hall*, 35 *Law Journal, Magistrates' Cases*, p. 251 (1866); 1 L. R. Q. B., p. 632. The statute 5 and 6 Will. IV., c. 74, enacted that no suit or other proceeding for the recovery of tithes and oblations under that amount should be instituted in any of his Majesty's courts in England then having cognisance of such matters, except in cases in which the title to such tithes, oblations, &c., was *bonâ fide* in question. An amending statute, 4 and 5 Vict., c. 36, took away the jurisdiction of the ecclesiastical courts in all cases in which the offerings sued for did not exceed £10. As the sums due for Easter offerings are generally small in amount, the recovery in a summary manner before two Justices of the Peace is in practice now the only mode available, except in cases of disputed title, which would come before the High Court.

Easter Offerings and Income Tax.

The question of the liability of Easter Offerings (in the popular sense of voluntary gifts at Easter) to Income Tax was long in doubt; but in the case of *Cooper* v. *Blakiston*,

[1907] 1 K. B., p. 336, and *Times* Law Report, December 12, 1906, Mr. Justice Bray decided that they were not assessable.

Fees at Archidiaconal Visitations.

" Clerical Mouse " asks for information as to the fees charged at archidiaconal visitations, whether they are anything but a voluntary offering, who benefits by them, and whether (1) he and (2) his churchwardens are bound to pay them.

1. As regards fees due from the clergy to the Archdeacon at his visitation, these are the ancient fees known as "procurations." In *Saunderson* v. *Claggett*, 1 Peere Williams's *Reports*, p. 656, 1 Strange's *Reports*, p. 420 (1720), it is laid down that—

"Of common right procurations are due to the Ordinary or Archdeacon. . . . Formerly the Visitor demanded a proportion of meat and drink for his refreshment when he came abroad to do his duty, and examine the state of the church. Afterwards these were turned into annual payments of a certain sum, which is called a procuration, being so much given to the Visitor *ad procurandum cibum et potum.*"

The court decided, *inter alia*, " that this was an ecclesiastical duty, and, therefore, properly suable for in the spiritual court." The clergy cannot escape from these fees, payment of which can be enforced by a sequestration order in the Consistory Court.

2. As regards the fees due from churchwardens, the law now rests upon the statute 30 and 31 Vict., c. 135, under which, in accordance with the Act, a table of fees has been fixed by Order in Council, and published in *The London Gazette*. This table, which will be found set out in full in Dale's *Clergyman's Legal Handbook*, seventh

edition, 1898, at pp. 449, 450, and in an abbreviated form in Phillimore's *Ecclesiastical Law*, Vol. II., p. 1059, and in Blunt's *Church Law*, seventh edition, 1894, p. 262, fixes the fee due to the Vicar-General, Chancellor, Archdeacon, or official at an episcopal or archidiaconal visitation at 2*s.*, the fee due to registrar or other officer by usage performing the duty at 12*s.* 6*d.*, and the fee due to the apparitor at 3*s.* 6*d.* It is explained in the Order in Council that—

"The Chancellor's fee includes the attendance of the Chancellor or his surrogate, the examination of the presentments of the outgoing churchwardens, and the admission of the new churchwardens to office. The registrar's fee includes the drawing and issuing of the inhibition and of the mandate for the citation of the clergy, the preparation of the visitation books and of the articles of inquiry, and the presentment papers, the attendance at the visitation and attesting the presentments and declarations of the churchwardens, the registering the papers exhibited by the clergy, the tabulating in the registry the copies of the register books of baptisms and burials and other papers required to be annually transmitted. The apparitor's fee includes the preparation and delivery of the citations to the clergy and churchwardens, and the attendance at the visitation."

The right of the registrar of an archdeaconry court to recover fees for attendance at the Archdeacon's visitation from the churchwardens of the parishes visited was affirmed by the Court of Common Pleas and the Exchequer Chamber in the case of *Shephard* v. *Payne*, 12 Common Bench N. S., p. 414 (1862); 16 *ib.*, p. 132; 31 L. J., Common Pleas, p. 297; 33 *ib.*, p. 158 (1864). In *Veley* v. *Pertwee*, L. R. 5 Q. B., p. 573 (1870), after the passing of the Compulsory Church Rate Abolition Act, 1868, it was held that churchwardens are not liable to pay the fee of the registrar due upon a visitation of the Archdeacon if they have no funds in hand available for the purpose. (*Vide supra*, pp. 31, 36.) But unless the churchwardens can satisfy the Archdeacon or his official that they are *bonâ fide* without means to pay, they must pay the legal fees demanded. Churchwardens, of course, incur no *personal* liability in the matter.

General.

Right of Lay Rector to Seats in Chancel.

Two questions have been asked in relation to the right of a lay rector to seats in the chancel for his family and friends :—

1. Can a lay rector claim seats in addition to the one seat set apart for his own use?

2. In case he appropriates seats to which he is not entitled, what is the remedy against him?

1. The rector, whether lay or spiritual, is entitled of common right to the " chief seat " in the chancel.—*Hall* v. *Ellis*, Noy's *Reports*, p. 133 (1610); *Spry* v. *Flood*, 2 Curteis, at p. 357. "The general rule," says Bayley, J., in *Clifford* v. *Weeks*, 1 Barnewall and Alderson's *Reports*, at p. 506 (1818)—

" Is that the rector is entitled to the principal pew in the chancel : but that the Ordinary may grant permission to other persons to have pews there."

"Seats in the chancel," says Bishop Gibson (*Codex*, ed. 1761, p. 200), "are under the disposition of the Ordinary, in like manner as those in the body of the church."

The meaning of " chief seat " came under consideration in *Stileman-Gibbard* v. *Wilkinson*, [1897] 1 Q. B., p. 749; *Times* Law Reports, Vol XIII., p. 145 :—

" The right to the chief seat," said Mr. Justice Charles,

"appears to be something more than a right to one sitting only. The size and situation of the seat must in each case, I presume, be determined by user" [1897] 1 Q. B. at p. 762.

The extent of the right, therefore, rests upon user, and it will be found in many cases that the lay rector is entitled to as many seats as may be required for the accommodation of himself, his family, and servants, and even in some cases his tenants. But, except in the case of pews which he holds by faculty, or claims by prescription, he cannot prevent the churchwardens as officers of the Ordinary from allotting seats to other persons in the chancel.

2. Should the lay rector attempt to obstruct the churchwardens in the performance of this duty, proceedings should be taken against him for "indecent behaviour" under the Brawling Act, 23 and 24 Vict., c. 32. If he goes further and tampers with the structure of the seats, by removal or otherwise, an action for trespass at the suit of the churchwardens would lie against him. If there is any dispute as to his title to a particular seat, the churchwardens should proceed to allot the seats in the ordinary way, leaving the lay rector to make good his claim by legal proceedings, if he can.

Spiritual Oversight of an Orphanage.

A correspondent inquires with reference to an orphanage in his parish—

"Supported by public contribution, professing to belong to the Church of England, and regulated by a committee of laymen, who have hitherto appointed as chaplain a priest who is not even licensed in the diocese"—

1. Whether he as parish priest has *ex officio* jurisdiction

over the souls of the inmates of such an establishment and the exclusive right to impart spiritual instruction to them.

2. What steps, if he is right in so contending, he ought to take to prevent a priest from intruding into his parish.

The law, as it stood unmodified by modern statutes, is clear. Dr. Lushington, in *Williams* v. *Brown*, 1 Curteis, at p. 56 (1835), lays it down that—

"It is not competent for the Ordinary himself without consent of the incumbent to license any person to officiate within the limits of the parish of that incumbent."

And the same learned judge, in *Hodgson* v. *Dillon*, 2 Curteis, p. 388 (1840), says:—

"The licence granted by the Bishop [to the minister of a proprietary chapel within the parish] emanates from his Episcopal authority. He could not, however, grant such a licence without the consent of the rector or vicar of the parish, for the cure of souls belongs exclusively to the rector or vicar."

And in *Freeland* v. *Neale*, 1 Robertson's *Ecclesiastical Reports*, p. 643 (1848), Sir H. Jenner-Fust ruled that a clergyman conducting service in the chapel of an almshouse without licence from the Bishop could not screen himself behind the contention that the inmates constituted a private family, and that his ministrations were not a "*public* reading of the prayers":—

"By the general law," said that learned judge, "no clergyman can daily officiate in the parish of another without his authority as well as that of the Bishop of the diocese" (at p. 649).

In these and other cases the cure of souls is recognised as conferring an exclusive right of ministration, which even the Bishop cannot invade without the incumbent's consent.

But the Private Chapels Act, 1871, 34 and 35 Vict., c. 66, gives power to—

" The Bishop of the diocese within which any chapel belonging to any college, school, hospital, asylum, or public or charitable institution is situated, whether consecrated or unconsecrated," to " license a clergyman of the Church of England to serve such chapel, and administer therein the Sacrament of the Lord's Supper, and perform such other offices and services of the Church of England as shall be specified in such licence."

And section 2 of the same Act enacts that a minister so licensed shall be—

" Subject to no control or interference on the part of the incumbent of the parish or district in which such chapel is situate."

It would seem that the institution in question comes within the scope of this Act, and that the Bishop has power to license a clergyman to officiate at the orphanage, if he sees fit. But apparently he has not availed himself of the power, and, so long as no clergyman has been duly and regularly licensed under the Act, the incumbent appears to be right in his contention that he, and he alone, has the spiritual oversight of the orphanage. To vindicate his right it would be necessary for him to take proceedings against the intruding clergyman in the Consistory Court under the Church Discipline Act, 1840, 3 and 4 Vict., c. 86. But as the Bishop has a discretion under that Act as to whether he would allow the suit to go forward, and can moreover render the proceedings nugatory by simply granting a licence in the manner already described, the incumbent would be ill advised to embark on such a course. The position of the clergyman appointed to act as chaplain by the committee of management is irregular ; but the Bishop has power to license him or any other clergyman to the post, if he thinks fit, even against the will of the incumbent.

Status of Perpetual Curates.

A correspondent asks (1) what legal rights and authority has a vicar, who is both instituted and inducted, more than a perpetual curate, who is merely instituted ? (2) Does the ceremony of the placing of the hand on the key of the church and the ringing of the bell bestow any legal rights beyond those conferred by institution ?

1. Generally speaking and apart from special local circumstances, the position of a perpetual curate differs in no way from that of a vicar. By 1 Geo. I., statute 2, cap. 10, all churches, curacies, or chapels augmented by the Governors of Queen Anne's Bounty were declared to be perpetual cures and benefices, and the ministers duly nominated and licensed thereunto were to be and be esteemed in law bodies politic and corporate with perpetual succession and a legal capacity to hold lands, tithes, &c. By 31 and 32 Vict., c. 117, s. 2, the incumbents of certain parishes, authorised to perform all the usual offices of the Church and to take the fees arising therefrom, were, for the purpose of style and designation, but not for any other purpose, to be deemed and styled vicars of such parishes. Perpetual curates, though now styled vicars, and sometimes instituted as such, are rightly only licensed. *Vide* Phillimore's *Eccl. Law*, Vol. I., p. 365 :—

" It only remains to mention that a perpetual curate is put in possession of his benefice by licence from the Bishop without either institution or induction."

After licence under the statute of George I. he is in as

full possession of his benefice as a vicar or rector who comes in by institution and induction.

2. Institution is a spiritual, induction a temporal act. *Vide* Johnson's *Clergyman's Vade Mecum*, ed. 1731, p. 81:—

"The clerk by institution has the cure of souls committed to him, and is answerable for neglect in this point."

"Induction is nothing else but the putting of the person into actual possession of the church and glebe, which are the temporalities of the Church; or the making of a complete incumbent of a church" (Godolphin, *Repertorium Canonicum*, ed. 1680, p. 278).

"By the institution the parson hath only *jus ad rem*, he hath not *jus in re* until he hath induction" (*ibid.*, p. 276).

Cf. Gibson's *Codex*, ed. 1761, Vol. II., p. 814; Title xxxiv., cap. 9, *Rules of Canon and Common Law concerning the manner and effects of induction*:—

"After institution the clerk is not complete incumbent till induction, or, as the Canon Law calls it, corporal possession. For by this it is that he becomes seised of the temporalities of the Church, so as to have power to grant them, or sue for them; . . . and by consequence, the church is completely full and the clerk is complete incumbent or possessor. On which accounts, it is compared in the books of Common Law to *livery* and *seisin*, by which possession is given of temporal estates."

This is the meaning of placing the hand upon the key, or upon the ring of the church door, or—

"If the key cannot be had, and there is no ring on the door, or if the church be ruinated, then on any part of the wall of the church or churchyard" (Phillimore, *Eccl. Law*, Vol. I., p. 359).

"In virtue of collation, as well as of institution, the clerk may enter into the glebe, and take the tithes; though, for want of induction, he cannot yet grant or sue for them" (*ibid.*, p. 357).

As will have been seen, by institution the benefice is full for most purposes; by induction certain temporal rights are superadded. Where an incumbent has patronage to administer, the right to present would presumably vest in him from the date when he himself received the cure of souls—*i.e.*, at institution.

Status of Curates.

Section 95 of the Pluralities Act, 1838, 1 and 2 Vict., c. 106, empowers an incumbent—

"Having first obtained the permission of the Bishop of the diocese, to be signified by writing under his hand, to require any one or more of his curates ... to quit and give up his curacy upon six months' notice thereof given to the curate, who shall thereupon quit the same according to such notice."

This section gives the curate no right to a hearing before the Bishop comes to a decision, and no right of appeal to the Archbishop of the province. It is not necessary that any charge should be made against the curate; it is enough that the Bishop in his discretion sees fit to remove him from the particular sphere of work to which he had been licensed. If the Bishop proceeds to revoke his licence, the curate has a right to be heard and an appeal to the Archbishop under section 98. But, short of revocation of the licence, the curate has no remedy.

"The object of the statute," said Lord Cranworth in *Poole* v. *Bishop of London*, 7 *Jurist, New Series*, at p. 348, "evidently is to authorise and compel the Bishop, for the benefit of the community, to exercise his discretion, in a summary way, on various matters in which it is necessary or expedient that a discretionary power should be lodged somewhere."

PAYMENT OF PARISH CLERK.

A correspondent puts the following case :—

"In an ancient parish in which there is no endowment of any kind to pay the parish clerk, if a majority of the ratepayers at the Easter vestry appoint a certain salary for the clerk against the wishes of the vicar and the vicar's warden, how can the latter guard themselves at the vestry against being held responsible, and possibly sued in the County Court, for such salary?"

Since the passing of the Compulsory Church Rate Abolition Act, 31 and 32 Vict., c. 109, the vestry has no power, except by levying a voluntary rate, a proceeding which is practically obsolete, to bind the churchwardens by a resolution of the kind suggested. Before the passing of that Act it was competent to the majority of a vestry to pay a salary to the parish clerk out of the Church rate, (vide Kemp v. *Attenborough* (1857), 30 *Law Times* (O.S.), p. 211, and 25 *Justice of the Peace*, p. 627), and a parish clerk could sue the churchwardens for neglecting to levy a rate, or, having levied it, for not having paid over what was due to him.—*Vide Parker* v. *Clerk* (1704), 3 Salkeld's *King's Bench Reports*, p. 87; 6 *Modern Reports*, p. 252. It should be noted that, if a voluntary rate be resorted to, any person making default in paying the amount for which he is rated is *ipso facto* disqualified under section 8 of the Act from "inquiring into, objecting to, or voting in respect of the expenditure of the moneys arising from such Church rate." Any factious or vexatious attempt on the part of the majority at the vestry to force the hands of the vicar and his warden may, therefore, safely be trusted to defeat itself. Either they must pay the money out of their own pockets or they forfeit their right to any voice in the matter. The funds, if any, in the churchwardens' hands are presumably the voluntary offerings of those who attend the church, and these the vicar and his warden cannot be compelled to appropriate to any particular object favoured by the vestry. In case of disagreement between the two churchwardens as to the distribution of alms, recourse must be had to the Ordinary.

Parish clerks, according to Canon 91—

"Shall have and receive their ancient wages, without fraud or diminution, either at the hands of the churchwardens, at such times as hath been accustomed, or by their own collection, according to the most ancient custom of every parish."

If in the parish in question any "ancient wages" have been accustomably due, the clerk would have his remedy at Common Law against the churchwardens; but in the case supposed of a vote by the vestry no action would lie, as on the side of the vestry there is no party capable of entering into a contract. The vicar, in any event, unless he personally contracts with the clerk, is exempt from liability. The case presents one more illustration of the unsatisfactory and illogical state of the law in which the passing of the Compulsory Church Rate Abolition Act resulted.

Payment of Tithes by one Vicar to Another.

A correspondent raises the following question :—"The vicar of A has glebe in the parish of B. Is such glebe legally chargeable with tithe to the vicar of B?"

Generally speaking, and apart from any local custom or prescription *in non decimando*, such glebe is titheable. *Vide* Eagle on the *Law of Tithes* (1830), Vol. I., p. 490 :—

"It has been made a question whether the maxim of *ecclesia ecclesiae decimas solvere non debet* applies to glebe-lands lying in another parish. It does not appear that this question has ever been judicially determined. The point was raised in a case before Lord Chief Baron Richards in 1817 [*The Warden and Minor Canons of St. Paul's* v. *the Dean of St. Paul's*, 3 Eagle and Younge's *Tithe Cases* at p. 813, 4 Price's *Exchequer Reports* at p. 77—a case in which the Warden and Minor Canons, as parsons of St. Gregory, sued the Dean of St. Paul's for tithes due in respect of the deanery house], who expressed a clear opinion, although he did not decide the point, that the maxim merely applies to a rector or vicar of the same church and parish, 'where the *ecclesia* would be paying tithes to itself ; as, where the rector or vicar is in possession of glebe, neither shall pay tithe to the other in respect of such occupation' ; and he referred to Watson's *Clergyman's Law*, ed. 1747, p. 513, where it is said, 'Though glebe-land, in itself considered, be all titheable as other lands be, yet no tithes shall be paid of the glebe by the parson [*i.e.*, impropriator] of a church to the vicar of the same church, whilst they are in the hands of the parson himself.'"

The Lord Chief Baron in his judgment goes on to say :—

"But there is no doubt that when the glebe of one clergyman is in the parish of another it must pay tithe; for that sort of privilege is confined to the clergy of the same parish."

Eagle endeavours to qualify this *dictum*, but there appears to be no doubt that it is a correct statement of the law.

Transmission of Copies of Parochial Registers.

A correspondent inquires whether incumbents are "in duty bound, as formerly, to forward transcripts of baptisms and burials annually to the diocesan registry, or more properly to hand them in through their churchwardens at the visitation."

The law rests on section 7 of 52 George III., c. 146, which enacted that copies of the register-books of baptisms, marriages, and burials, duly verified and attested, should be transmitted by the churchwardens to the registrar of the diocese by post, on or before June 1st in every year. But so long ago as 1832 a Royal Commission reported that "in consequence of the imperfections in the details of this Act, and the want of adequate remuneration for the duties imposed, these copies are not transmitted with regularity."—*Vide* Stephens's *Ecclesiastical Statutes*, Vol. I., p. 1033, footnote (1).

It appears that the legal obligation has been very generally disregarded of late years, possibly in consequence of the more careful registration of births and deaths by the State than prevailed when the Act was passed. Some bishops are much more particular on the point than others. A visitation is not the proper time for handing in the copies.

Repair of Family Tomb in a Churchyard.

Q.—A. B., who possesses a family vault in an ancient parish churchyard, and is the last of his line, inquires:

(1) "Whether he can legally leave a sum of money to be invested in Consols or other securities, the interest thereof to be paid yearly to the vicar and churchwardens

for the time being of the parish in which the vault is situated upon trust to pay the sexton, or some other person, to cut the grass within the enclosure, to paint the railings every third year, and to keep the memorial in repair?"

(2) " Whether, if this proposal cannot legally be carried out, there is any means whereby the memorial can be maintained in perpetuity by leaving a sum of money for that express purpose?"

A.—(1) There are numerous cases which establish that money cannot lawfully be left for the repair of a tomb in a *churchyard*, because the gift is not "charitable" in the legal sense, and violates the rule against perpetuities. It will suffice to mention the cases of *Rickard* v. *Robson*, 31 Beavan's *Reports*, p. 244, and *Hoare* v. *Osborne*, L. R. 1 Equity, p. 585. In the case of *Pirbright* v. *Salwey*, *Weekly Notes*, 1896, p. 86, it was held by Stirling, J., "that a bequest to the rector and churchwardens of a sum of money to be applied, so long as the aw for the time being permitted, to the repair of a grave in a churchyard was valid for at least a period of twenty-one years from the death of the testator." A bequest to maintain a tomb *inside* the church, or so placed that it forms part of the fabric of the church, is good because it is for the benefit of the inhabitants generally, and therefore "charitable."—*Vide* Tudor's *Charitable Trusts*, fourth ed. (1906), pp. 53 and 54.

(2) There is a method whereby A. B. can effect his purpose. In the case of *In re Tyler*, [1891] 3 Chancery, p. 252, it was held by the same learned judge, and affirmed in the Court of Appeal, that the bequest of a sum of money to the trustees of a charity with a proviso that, if they should at any time neglect to keep in repair the testator's family vault in Highgate cemetery, the

money should be paid over to another charity, was valid. A. B. should bequeath a sufficient sum to the trustees of some local charity with a "gift over" to some other charity recognised by the law, in case they should neglect to keep the vault in repair in the manner specified in his will. The bequest should be sufficient in amount to induce the trustees to accept the legacy.

Fees for Monuments in Churches.

A correspondent inquires whether, in a case in which no custom can be shown to exist regulating the fees payable for the erection of monuments in the church, the incumbent can decide the amount of the fee "at his own discretion and according to his own exigencies."

There is some conflict of authority on the question, the answer to which would depend upon the particular circumstances in each case ; *e.g.*, whether it was proposed to erect the monument in the chancel or the body of the church, upon the *status* of the incumbent, whether he was rector or vicar, whether there was a lay rector, and so forth. Upon the general question Lord Stowell, in *Maidman* v. *Malpas*, 1 Haggard's *Consistory Reports*, at p. 208 (1794), thus states the law :—

"The permission of the Ordinary is necessary before any monument can properly be erected. It is to his care that the fabric of the church is committed, that it shall not be injured or deformed by the caprice of individuals. The consent of the incumbent is taken on such occasions, and especially of the rector for monuments in the chancel. A faculty likewise is required, though it is frequently omitted under the confidence reposed in the minister, and the Ecclesiastical Court is not eager to interfere. But when cases are brought before it, it is necessary to inquire whether the thing is proper to be done, and whether the consent of the incumbent has been obtained. . . .

"I conceive the clergyman may legally demand and accept a fee for his consent."

The same learned judge, in *Bardin* v. *Calcott*, 1 Haggard's *Consistory Reports*, p. 14 (1789), says, with regard to the payment of such fees :—

"It is no general Common Law right, but custom will interpose ; and where it is shown to be customary, such practice will be supported."

In *Rich* v. *Bushnell*, 4 Haggard's *Ecclesiastical Reports*, 164 (1827), a case in which the lay rector and owner of a chancel applied for a faculty to make a vault and erect tablets in the chancel, Sir John Nicholl, Dean of the Arches, thus expressed his view of the law :—

"It may be doubtful whether the consent of the vicar is necessary to the construction of a vault, or to the affixing of a tablet even in the body of the church, or whether he has in such a case a claim to a fee, unless where established by a special custom" (at p. 172).

And at p. 173 he adds :—

"This strange notion of payment for consent seems to spread, and to meet with no unwilling assent in some quarters, whereas no fee of the kind is due of common right ; it can only be due by special custom. If such a custom could have a reasonable foundation, it must at least be strictly proved, and this Court would not carry it one step beyond such proof ; the introduction of such a practice would be most dangerous ; and it would require very strong authority . . . to satisfy me that the vicar could, by custom, possess a right of refusing his consent to an interment in the chancel, *a fortiori*, to the grant of a faculty for a vault or a tablet, unless not a fixed but a reasonable fee is agreed to be paid."

In *Rugg* v. *Kingsmill*, L. R. 2 Privy Council, 59 (1868), another case in which an application by a lay rector for a faculty to make a vault under the chancel was opposed by the vicar, it was held by the Privy Council that—

"The vicar or perpetual curate, although entitled to officiate in and have free access to the chancel, has no right, strictly speaking, to fees for the erection of monumental tablets . . . in the chancel."

Mr. Brooke Little in the *Law of Burial*, third ed., p. 59, writes thus :—

"It is submitted that the parson's right to demand a fee for the erection of monuments in a churchyard or body of a church will, in the same manner as burial fees, depend upon custom."

The learned editor of Phillimore's *Ecclesiastical Law*, Vol. I., p. 692, following Burn's *Ecclesiastical Law*, Vol. I., p. 273, says of the erection of monuments in *churchyards* :—

"If the incumbent's leave is necessary for the erecting of a monument, it seems that he may prescribe his own reasonable terms ; or if an accustomed fee has been paid, that such custom ought to be observed."

The balance of authority seems to be against the incumbent's claim to an unfettered discretion as to the amount of the fee to be exacted in cases in which the amount is not fixed by custom. But where a custom to pay fees of some undetermined amount on the erection of monuments is proved, the incumbent would occupy strong ground in demanding a "reasonable" fee. If the demand were disputed, it would be for the judge or jury before whom the case might come to decide as to the reasonableness of the amount claimed.

It is assumed that the case in question is not complicated by the existence of a lay rector.

THE CONFIRMATION OF THE BISHOP-ELECT OF WORCESTER
(Dr. Charles Gore).

SUMMARY OF THE ARGUMENTS.

[*Reprinted, by permission of the proprietors, from the* Guardian *of February* 5 *and* 12, 1902.]

[*Prefatory Note.*—The Rev. Charles Gore, Canon of Westminster, was, under *congé d'élire* and letter missive of the King, elected by the Dean and Chapter of Worcester to the See of Worcester on Dec. 21, 1901. The election having been certified to the Archbishop of Canterbury and the Royal assent obtained, the Archbishop, by his Vicar-General, C. A. Cripps, K.C., proceeded to confirm the election at the Church House, Westminster, on January 22, 1902. A notice had previously been posted on the doors of the Church House requiring objectors to state their objections in writing beforehand, and stating that the Vicar-General would consider these at a sitting in Chambers. This constituted a departure from the established order of procedure. The Vicar-General first sat in Chambers, after which objectors were publicly cited, but on coming forward were informed that their objections could not be heard, and the confirmation then proceeded in the usual form, with the exception that the objectors were publicly called once only. Rules *nisi* having been obtained on behalf of two of the objectors, A. W. Cobham and E. H. Garbett, the Archbishop of Canterbury and the Vicar-General appeared to show cause why a writ of *mandamus* should not issue commanding them to hear and determine the objections. The arguments were heard on February 3, 4, and 5, and the judgments were delivered on February 10, 1902. *Vide Rex* v. *Archbishop of Canterbury*, [1902] 2 K. B., pp. 503–512.]

Monday, February 3rd.

After an interval of exactly fifty-four years, the question of the power of a Metropolitan to hold an inquiry into the fitness of a person nominated by the Crown, and

POINTS OF CHURCH LAW 65

elected under compulsion by the Dean and Chapter of a vacant see, to be his suffragan, once more came under judicial review in the King's Courts. It cannot be asserted that feeling on the second occasion ran so high, or that the proceedings were taken in quite such deadly earnest, as they were in the case of Bishop Hampden, which ended in so lame and impotent a conclusion in 1848.[1] Nevertheless, the densely crowded appearance of the court when the Lord Chief Justice, accompanied by Mr. Justice Wright and Mr. Justice Ridley, took his seat on the Bench on the morning of Monday, February 3, bore witness to the very keen interest felt by persons of very diverse views in Church and State in the legal, constitutional, and canonical questions on which issue was joined.

Certainly if justice is best secured to the Church of England by entrusting her interests to the dispassionate handling of persons the most remote in sympathy and by training from Anglican orthodoxy, the desired result could hardly have been better attained. It was remarked with some amusement that of the formidable phalanx of counsel engaged in the case, the Attorney-General, Sir Robert Finlay, was a Scotchman; the Solicitor-General, Sir Edward Carson, was an Irishman, hailing from Ulster; Mr. Haldane, K.C., for the respondents, was also a Scotchman; Mr. Danckwerts, K.C., was of Cape Dutch extraction; while another of the learned counsel engaged was of Hebraic origin. The Vicar-General, Mr. Cripps, K.C., occupied a seat in the front row beside Sir Edward Clarke.

The *mise en scène*, if the phrase be permissible, had been transferred since 1848 from Westminster to the

---

[1] The Judges of the Queen's Bench were equally divided, Coleridge and Patteson, JJ., being in favour of the rule being made absolute, Denman, C.J., and Erle, J., against.—*Vide* Jebb's *Hampden Case*, pp. 443-496, *Reg.* v. *Archbishop of Canterbury*, 11 Q.B. pp. 564-666.

Strand; the *dramatis personæ* in the earlier case were all dead and mostly forgotten; but the parts in this twentieth-century revival were curiously reversed. The extreme Protestant wing, then in closest alliance with the Whig Erastianism of the Ministers of the Crown, had become the attacking party, forced to rely on Canon Law and primitive practice; while the attacking force of those days, in uncomfortable alliance with the Crown, found itself entertaining a certain sympathy with the tactics and arguments of its ancient foes.

THE CASE FOR THE CROWN.

The *Attorney-General*,[1] in opening the case, first read the fateful statute 25 Henry VIII., c. 20, quite through from beginning to end, and then referred to a statute passed a year or two earlier, 23 Henry VIII., c. 20, which, reciting the evils due to the practice of Bishops-elect having to go to Rome to obtain Bulls for Confirmation, provided for nomination by the King straight away in case of delay. Under the later statute the Dean and Chapter were bound to elect the person mentioned in the King's Letters Missive within twelve days, failing which the King was empowered to nominate by Letters Patent, whereupon the Archbishop was bound to proceed at once to the consecration. In the former case the King was to signify the election to the Archbishop, requiring and commanding him to confirm, invest, and consecrate the Bishop-elect. Section 7 provides that if the Archbishop does not

[1] Counsel for the Crown were the Attorney-General, Sir R. B. Finlay, K.C., the Solicitor-General, Sir E. H. Carson, K.C., Mr. Dibdin, K.C., and Mr. H. Sutton; for the Archbishop of Canterbury, Sir E. Clarke, K.C., and Mr. E. W. Hansell; for the Bishop-elect, Mr. G. J. Talbot, and Mr. Rayner Goddard; for the respondent Cobham, Mr. Haldane, K.C., Mr. Bramwell Davis, K.C., and Mr. Whitehead; for the respondent Garbett, Mr. Danckwerts, K.C., and Mr. Morton Smith.

within twenty days confirm, invest, and consecrate, he shall be liable to the penalties of *praemunire*. Their lordships, said *Sir R. Finlay*, in construing the statute would naturally look to what was the state of the law before the statute. He quoted a number of authorities to show that before the statute of Henry VIII. there had been very great fluctuation. There were two parties to the transaction, the King and the Pope. Whatever might have been the process in earlier days, from the time of Edward III. onwards the Pope had drawn to himself the right of Confirmation. The last instance of Confirmation in England in pre-Reformation times was the case of Wakeryng, appointed to the see of Norwich in 1416, and confirmed by the Metropolitan under the short-lived temporary statute, 3 Henry V., passed to meet the difficulties occasioned by the Great Schism in the Papacy. To show that Confirmation under the statute was intended to be a mere form, the *Attorney-General* referred to the statute 31 Henry VIII., c. 9, which created six new bishoprics,[1] to which the King presented by Letters Patent. It was inconceivable, he argued, that the result arrived at should be so very different in the two cases as it would be if in the one case the King's nomination was to be subject to review by the Archbishop at Confirmation. Election was followed by Confirmation as part of one and the same act. It would be said by his learned friends that the Archbishop had the duty of examining the Bishop-elect, and that Confirmation by the Archbishop was an essential part of the proper procedure. He would refer their lordships to a number of instances in which Confirmation was dispensed with altogether. There was, first, the case of the Dean and Chapter refusing to elect. Then there were the new bishoprics created under 31 Henry

[1] Bristol, Chester, Gloucester, Oxford, Peterborough, and Westminster.

VIII., c. 9. Lastly, there was the case of the Suffragan Bishops appointed under 26 Henry VIII., c. 14. The fact that no Confirmation was required in any of these cases went far to destroy the argument from the supposed necessity of Confirmation under the Canon Law. He referred also to the Irish statute, 2 Eliz., c. 4, which, reproducing the language of 1 Edward VI., c. 2, subsequently repealed and not revived, characterised the elections of Archbishops and Bishops by Deans and Chapters as being "in very deed no elections," but only "colours, shadows, and pretences of elections, serving to no purpose, and seeming also derogatory and prejudicial to the King's prerogative royal," abolished elections, and enacted that the Queen might by her Letters Patent confer the same upon any person whom she should think to be meet; to as much and the same effect as though a *congé d'élire* had issued.[1] The learned Attorney seemed to press the Irish analogy rather far, repeatedly alluding to the English and Irish Churches as one United Church, and apparently forgetting that they had an entirely separate existence down to 1801, and were united under the Act of Union for the short space of only seventy years. He cited the case of *O'Brian* v. *Knivan*, Cro. Jac. 552, in support of his argument, in which a lease granted by a Bishop intruded into the see of Ossory by Queen Mary in the lifetime of a former Bishop, appointed by Edward VI. by Letters Patent, was held void on the ground that the earlier appointment was valid, the King having power to appoint by Letters Patent without any *congé d'élire*, "which is but a form or ceremony which the kings of

---

[1] The reason for the abandonment of the *congé d' élire* in Ireland was that the disaffected Irish chapters could not be trusted to elect the Crown's nominees. *Vide* Ball's *Reformed Church of Ireland* (1886), Chapter iv. p. 59. The Irish Bishops continued to be appointed by Letters Patent until the disestablishment.

this realm have agreed to observe." Referring to modern legislation erecting bishoprics in England in places where no Dean and Chapter existed, to the case of India and the Crown Colonies, he contended that all these cases, in which Confirmation was out of the question, absolutely annihilated the arguments which might be adduced to prove that Confirmation was a living thing. As to post-Reformation usage, the only recorded instance of opposition at Confirmation prior to that of Bishop Hampden in 1848 was the case of the Confirmation of Bishop Mountague to the see of Chichester in 1629, when "one Jones, a bookseller, attended with the mob," charging him "with Popery, Arminianism, and other heterodoxies," which came to nothing.

A discussion then took place between the *Lord Chief Justice* and the *Attorney-General* as to the position of the Vicar-General, the Attorney-General seeking to prove by a long array of authorities that the matters within the Vicar-General's cognisance, including Confirmation, were merely formal and non-contentious. He referred at some length to the fifteenth and sixteenth century Canonists, Lancelottus and Ferrari, only to brush them aside as irrelevant and inapplicable to procedure under the statute. Having cited in favour of his view of the statute the opinions of such eminent civilians as Dr. Lushington, Dr. Burnaby, and Sir John Dodson in the Hampden case, and of Sir Travers Twiss in Dr. Temple's case in 1869, he concluded with the words :—

"I do most strenuously submit that beyond the points of the validity of the election and the identity of the person elected no objection of any kind can be entertained."

The *Attorney-General* resumed his seat at a few minutes after three, and was followed by the *Solicitor-General*, Sir E. Carson, who confined himself entirely to the legal construction of the statute and the absurdities which he maintained would flow from the construction sought to be put upon it. When election by the Dean and Chapter had taken place, that election, by the terms of the statute, shall stand good and effectual to all intents and purposes. If the election so stands good, is not that conclusive that Confirmation is a mere form? It was natural enough that forms should be kept up at a time of contention between the King and the Pope, between the clergy and the Crown, between the clergy and the people. The King in his Letters Missive described the qualities of the person to be elected. It was for the King and his advisers, not for the Archbishop, to determine whether the nominee had the proper qualities. If they were to read all that they found in Lancelottus and the rest into English Statute Law, they would be going further than had ever been done before. Warned by certain protestations in the Hampden case, he would take particular pains not to use the expression a *sham*, but if the view contended for on the other side was the right one, the King might as well abrogate his right to nominate altogether. He submitted that the Vicar-General was right in his ruling, and that there was no power in the Archbishop.

Mr. Dibdin, K.C., contended that the objections put forward did not appear to charge the Bishop-elect with any ecclesiastical offence at all. To say that a man's writings had given pain to a certain number of persons in tbe Church was not to charge him with an ecclesiastical offence. Even if the case for the Crown were all wrong, how could his learned friends obtain a *mandamus* when their own case disclosed no ecclesiastical offence? The strength and force of the case put forward by the other side was that it was a matter of essence that in the appointment of a Bishop the election should be confirmed by the authority of the Metropolitan. But how could this be in view of the fact that above 100 Bishops of the Church of England do not require Confirmation? Not more than twenty-five Bishops all told can be subject to the process of Confirmation. What became, then, of the remaining three-fourths? Election was a form, Confirmation was a form. It was impossible to give a vigour and force and influence to one form which is not in the other, and which is in terms denied by the statute.

This concluded the case for the Crown.

Sir E. Clarke was proceeding to address the Court for the Archbishop of Canterbury when the adjournment took place.

Sir E. Clarke for the Archbishop of Canterbury.

Tuesday, February 4th.

When the Court rose on Monday afternoon *Sir E. Clarke* was arguing the point that neither Captain Cobham nor Mr. Garbett had any *locus standi*, any "interest" in the legal sense of the term, in the case at all. Captain Cobham had not appeared at the Church House, nor had he lodged any objection beforehand in writing, as required in the citation of the Vicar-General. Mr. Garbett, it was true, had complied with these formalities, but he had no connexion with the diocese of Worcester, and had shown no "interest." *Sir Edward* was returning to the point to-day, when the *Lord Chief Justice* intimated that if he felt bound to press it, and if their lordships should be of opinion that the technical objection was good, there would be an end of the present proceedings. The flaw would doubtless be set right by counsel for the objectors moving for a new rule on behalf of persons who had a legal interest, with the result that the arguments would have to be heard over again. After consultation with the Attorney-General and the other counsel for the Crown, *Sir E. Clarke* said that he would not insist upon the point. He then read the Archbishop's commission to the Vicar-General, and cited a number of authorities to show that as Vicar-General he is not a judicial officer. He read the judgments of Dr. Burnaby and Dr. Lushington, delivered at Bow Church, in the Hampden case, and submitted that, taken together with the divided opinion of the Court of Queen's Bench, their authority was very strong. There was a stream of authority in favour of the view of the statute, 25 Henry VIII., c. 20, for which he was contending. All the words of the statute were mandatory, and the Archbishop was subjected to penalties if he did not comply. As to the passage which had been cited from the Bishops' Book and the King's Book, published in 1537 and 1543 respectively, the passage did not apply to Confirmation at all, but to incumbencies in the diocese. There had taken its place the most explicit assertion of the King's authority, as a very interesting passage in the works of Archbishop Cranmer, published by the Parker Society, plainly showed.[1] In the case before the court he would remind their lordships of what actually happened. Certain persons came and stated their objections. They were objections to doctrine, which did not specify any

---

[1] "The ministers of God's word under his majesty be the bishops, parsons, vicars, and such other priests as be appointed by his highness to that ministration . . . . All the said officers and ministers . . . . be appointed, assigned, and elected in every place, by the laws and orders of kings and princes."

"In the admission of many of these officers be divers comely ceremonies and solemnities used, which be not of necessity, but only for a good order and seemly fashion; for if such offices and ministrations were committed without such solemnity they were nevertheless truly committed." *Remains and Letters*, p. 116.

POINTS OF CHURCH LAW 73

particular heresy on the part of the Bishop-elect, but were mere suggestions that he was not a fit and proper person to be a Bishop. Their claim was that the Archbishop should declare unfit a man whom the Crown had selected as fit for the office. Even if all the objections were heard, the Archbishop would have no judgment to give. Nothing of the kind was provided for. Supposing that the objectors were allowed to go through Canon Gore's books page by page and to allege all that they could against the religious societies to which he belonged, all the Archbishop had to do under the statute was to proceed to confirm the election. It was not true to say that Confirmation and Consecration were mere formalities. Confirmation was a process required to obtain the spiritualities of the see, Consecration followed with the most solemn questions addressed to the Bishop-elect, which were quite sufficient to safeguard purity of doctrine.

Mr. Hansell followed on the same side. If the opposers had any grievance, it was that having been cited to appear and state their objections, they were not permitted to appear in due form of law. The Vicar-General had proceeded with the Confirmation, which was exactly what the opposers were told would happen. The opposers were bound by the terms of the citation, which recited the Royal commands and the Archbishop's duty to proceed to Confirmation. There was an intimation that the Confirmation would be proceeded with whether opposers appeared or not. The Confirmation had proceeded strictly in terms of the citation.

Mr. Talbot for the Bishop-elect.

Mr. G. J. Talbot, for the Bishop-elect, said that his client desired to take up substantially the same position as he did at the Confirmation ceremony. The Bishop-elect did not feel that it would be becoming in him to argue against the Archbishop's power. He was, however, anxious that their lordships should know that he did not desire to avoid these questions, but was perfectly willing to meet them so far as was permissible by law. Further than that he did not desire to intervene in these proceedings.

THE CASE FOR THE RESPONDENTS.
Mr. Haldane's Argument.

Mr. Haldane, K.C., rose to address the court on behalf of Captain Cobham exactly at noon. There were three questions to be considered. What was the meaning and effect of 25 Henry VIII., c. 20 ? What was the position of things at the time when that statute was passed ? What light had been cast on the construction of the statute by subsequent usage ? The substance of the matter was, What was the nature of Confirmation ? Confirmation could not be separated from Consecration. From the earliest times a struggle had gone on between the temporal and the spiritual power. The placing of Bishops was in the hands of the temporal power, the making of Bishops was in the hands of the spiritual power. Consecration was the office by which the spiritual *status* came to the Bishop. If his learned friends were right, Confirmation and Consecration from early times were mere forms, and Confirmation was the idlest of idle ceremonies. The Attorney-General had spoken of forms where the substance had been changed while the outward semblance had been kept up. If that were so here, all that took place before the Archbishop, including Consecration, was an idle form. The *Lord Chief Justice*, interposing, said Mr. Haldane had no right to say that that applied to Consecration, to which *Mr. Haldane* answered that the statute gave equal prominence to Consecration and Confirmation. Continuing, the learned counsel said it was a fallacy to try to liken the jurisdiction of the Archbishop in Confirmation to the forms and proceedings in court. The Archbishop had a discretion which he was bound to exercise reasonably and according to the laws of the Church. Even if it were true, as had been said, that no ecclesiastical offence had been committed, he contended that that was totally irrelevant. The real meaning of Confirmation was that the person presented to a bishopric came before the Church to have his fitness tested. He then traced the history of the election and confirmation of Bishops in Europe from the earliest times, the people at first electing of their free choice and the Sovereign power afterwards stepping in, and showed that even in Anglo-Saxon times the King had obtained the control of the appointment of Bishops in England. The long struggle as to investiture followed, beginning with the dispute between Anselm and William Rufus, and the conflict, which had begun in the time of the Anglo-Saxon Kings, might be said to have come to a head at the time of the Reformation. It was common ground that from 1316, the date of the last opposed Confirmation, down to the passing of the statute in 1533, there was no recognised form of Confirmation in England. Rome had drawn to itself the jurisdiction of the Archbishop of the province, and the statute of Henry VIII. did but legalise a return to the normal state of things. It was not passed for the purpose of doing away with Confirmation, but it said that the ceremony should take place in the normal place, and not at Rome. It was passed solely to cut down the interference of Rome. The true theory was that Confirmation belonged to the Metropolitan, and was wrongfully usurped by Rome. The statute was designed to remedy this abuse. Mr. Haldane then referred to the preface to the Ordinal, written by Archbishop Cranmer, in which the words " first called, tried, and examined " pointed clearly to the reality of Confirmation. The real question, he said in conclusion, was not as to this and that detail; at the root of the matter lay the wider question to which he had confined his argument. If there was a real duty on the part of the Archbishop to consider these matters at Confirmation, opportunity ought to be given. If the Crown's construction of the statute was right, then not merely Confirmation but Consecration was reduced to a form; solemn they might be as ceremonies, interesting as historical survivals, but safeguards they were not.

Mr. Bramwell Davis followed on the same side, and had not concluded his argument when the court rose.

Mr. Bramwell Davis's Argument.

Wednesday, February 5th.

Mr. Bramwell Davis, K.C., resumed his argument on behalf of Captain Cobham on Wednesday. When the court rose on Tuesday he was arguing from the statute 3 Henry V., passed to remedy the disorders caused by the Papal schism, and the writs in Rymer's *Foedera* issued under that statute, that there had been a continuous practice in the form of Confirmation from 1316 down to the time of Henry VIII.:—

"Our point," said the learned counsel, "is this, that whenever there was a Confirmation of the election of the Bishop, it was a solemn judicial proceeding, whether taking place at Rome or before the Archbishop here; and in support of that, I say, look at the writs after the time of Henry V., and look at the writs at the time of Henry VIII., and I say you have a sustained practice although it is very difficult to find any authority, and I think there is very little really to show what took place in that interval of 200 years."

The real point of the Act of Henry VIII., he submitted, was to get rid of the authority of the Pope. Whether the King proceeded by Letters Patent or the Archbishop confirmed on election, in each case the Archbishop was to consecrate without getting any Bulls from Rome. It was the delays and exactions of Rome that were struck at. Under the statute the Archbishop was to confirm, "with all due circumstance," to invest and consecrate the Bishop-elect, and to "give and use to him pall, and all other benedictions, ceremonies and things requisite for the same." "Confirm," at the time of the passing of the statute, had a well defined meaning, according to the Common Law. To confirm the election of a Bishop meant with all due circumstance, and with all the rights and provisions of the Canon Law—*i.e.*, as providing something in the nature of a judicial decision. There was no doubt that the Canon Law, so far as it had become a part of the Common Law, was binding upon the judges of this country. As to the statute 1 Edward VI., c. 2, the statement in it that election by the Dean and Chapter was a sham, taken together with its silence as to Confirmation, strengthened his argument as to the meaning of the word "confirm." Coming to post-Reformation times, for a period undoubtedly of 300 years there had been a regular recognised practice in cases of Confirmation. He submitted that there must have been a recognised practice at the time of Henry VIII. How otherwise was the procedure which was found in existence in Archbishop Parker's case so soon after the passing of the statute to be accounted for? It seemed impossible to think that this practice could have been invented in Parker's case, the solemn citation of persons, the court being held, a petition being presented containing all these clauses, if the whole thing was a sham and intended to be a sham. The fact of all this solemn ritual being gone through pointed to its being intended to be a real thing at that time. There was in it every element of a judicial proceeding. Turning to the form itself, Mr. *Bramwell Davis* contended, on the authority of Bishop Gibson, that if there was no citation of opposers and the business was not discussed, the Confirmation was void. The opportunity given to opposers by the *Si quis* at the ordination of deacons and priests, and the absence of any such form in the service for the Consecration of a Bishop, led irresistibly to the conclusion that the inquiry in the former case was equivalent to the Confirmation which had already taken place in the case of a Bishop. He next referred to Nicholls' *Commentary on the Book of Common Prayer*, published in 1710, which, after setting forth the processes required under the statute, concluded with the words :—

"Whereupon the Archbishop and Bishops proceeding according to the ancient form, do cause all such as can object, either against the manner of election or person elected, to be cited to make their objections. When the validity of the election and *sufficiency* of the person are by public acts and due proceedings judicially approved, then follows consecration, &c."

Bishop Fell in 1669 wrote to much the same effect. Salkeld, too, in his third volume used the language : "Whereupon the Archbishop examines the election and the party, and then confirms the election and consecrates him."

In fact, so far as regarded the text writers and other learned persons writing on the question, there was almost a unanimity of authority on the point, with the doubtful exception of a note by Sir James Marriott, who was Vicar-General in 1764, until they reached the middle of the nineteenth century.

As to the jurisdiction of the Vicar-General, he contended that, even assuming that the Vicar-General could not deal with contentious matters, it would be his duty, whenever anything of a contentious nature arose, to refer the matter to the Archbishop, whose duty it was to undertake the Confirmation. The learned counsel concluded with the words :—

"If the Attorney-General's view is correct, the King now has an absolute right to nominate a Bishop in every case, not only in a case where there is no election provided for in the statute of Henry VIII., but in every case, because, if your lordships refuse the rule for a *mandamus*, there is no discretion in anybody to refuse to consecrate the nominee of the King. That is a serious question, and I submit to your lordships that supposing for instance after the election of a Bishop he changes his views and becomes a member of some other Church, still there is no discretion in the Archbishop, who would be bound to confirm that person and bound to consecrate him, provided he was able to answer merely the questions that are provided for in the consecration service. Is it to be said that no one has any discretion whatever to refuse to confirm and consecrate a Bishop whatever his religious views and whatever his conduct in the past may have been as to other subjects ? I submit with confidence that the rule ought to go in this case, and that the Archbishop always has had, and ought to have now, a discretion as to whether he will confirm the Bishop-elect or not."

Mr. Benjamin Whitehead followed on behalf of the same respondent. He referred to the absence of any statutory Ordinal between the dates 1533 and 1550. There was no Ordinal except the Roman Pontifical, and there was no difference as regards form between the forms for Consecration and Confirmation. Neither was contained in the statute-book, but you had to seek the forms elsewhere. He submitted there was no doubt that you had to go to the *jus commune* of the Church of Rome—*i.e.*, the common law of the Church of Rome, which governed the Church throughout Christendom. Recourse must have been had in the case of Consecration to the Roman Pontifical. Similarly Confirmation must have followed some then existing and well-recognised form. The pains taken under Elizabeth by the passing of 8 Eliz., c. 1, to set at rest all doubts as to the legality of ordinations performed without statutory authority under the Ordinal of Edward VI., repealed by Philip and Mary, showed the importance which was attached to these forms.

Mr. Danckwerts's Argument.

Mr. Danckwerts, K.C., then addressed the Court on behalf of the respondent Garbett. Dealing with the statute 1 Edward VI., c. 2, on the preamble to which his learned friends for the Crown had laid such stress, as characterising elections by the Dean and Chapter as "colours, shadows, and pretences of elections," he cited the authority of a learned German writer, Felix Makower, in a work on the *Constitutional History of the Church of England*, published in Berlin in 1895, to show that there was some virtue attaching to Confirmation in the opinion of the Parliament of Edward VI. The statute created an artificial state of things, which put the King's bare appointment in the same position as though there had been a *congé d'élire*, an election, and a Confirmation. If Confirmation was a mere ceremony, the Archbishop having no choice but to induct the King's nominee, why was the statute so careful and precise in its language? It was curious that the statute should think it necessary to enact that the King's appointment made under this statute should have the same form and effect as though there had been not only the *congé d'élire* and election, but also Confirmation.

Mr. Danckwerts next addressed himself to the question of the position of the Vicar-General:—

"My point," he said, "is this: This is the Metropolitical Court of the Archbishop, held there before the Archbishop himself or his Vicar-General, and it is the duty of the Vicar-General first to permit the opposers to appear, and then to bring in articles in the usual way."

When issue had been properly joined between the opposers and the Dean and Chapter, who by their proctor prayed Confirmation of the election, it was for the Vicar-General to try the case, or even to adjourn it to the Archbishop in the first instance. Whether the Vicar-General was himself to try, or the Archbishop, must depend upon the action of the Archbishop himself. In three early cases in the reign of Elizabeth the Archbishop himself had actually presided.[1] The Vicar-General sitting in this

---

[1] Archbishop Grindal presided in person at the confirmation of:—

(1) John Piers, Bishop of Rochester, translated to Salisbury and confirmed in that See, December 2, 1577.

(2) John Young, elected Bishop of Rochester. Election confirmed March 15th, 157$\frac{7}{8}$. *Vide* Archbishop Grindal's Register at Lambeth, pp. 35 and 42.

Archbishop Whitgift presided in person at the confirmation of Thomas Cowper, Bishop of Lincoln, translated to Winchester, and confirmed in that See, March 23, 158$\frac{3}{4}$. *Vide* Archbishop Whitgift's Register, Vol. I. p. 9. The formula in all these cases is:—

"In capella Reverendissimi in Christo patris et Domini Domini [*sic*] Edmundi [Johannis] divina providentia Cantuarien. Archiepiscopi totius Angliæ Primatis et Metropolitani infra Manorium suum de Lambehithe *coram eodem Reverendissimo patre.*"

The cases before the Vicar-General only were heard at St. Mary-le-Bow.

court had even tried cases of heresy. The learned counsel then read the Letters Patent of the Archbishop of Canterbury appointing Mr. Cripps to the office of Vicar-General, from which it appeared that authority had been committed to him " to discuss, decide, and finally to determine all manner of excesses and crimes of all and every the subjects living and residing as well within our diocese of Canterbury and our peculiar jurisdiction, as within our whole province of Canterbury," the correction, punishment, and reformation thereof, and " to correct, chastise, and to punish, and to enjoin them a proper and salutary penance for the crimes by them committed." The Letters Patent further stated :—

" And we do for us and our successors give and grant to you the authority above and full power with faculty of right, confirming all elections whatsoever of all Bishops of our province of Canterbury according to the exigency of the law, and of the statutes of the Kingdom of Great Britain . . . . with all lawful power of coercion," &c.

" I submit," said *Mr. Danckwerts*, " that that clearly shows that he has a contentious jurisdiction." In support of his argument he cited the cases of *Lucy v. the Bishop of St. David's*,[1] in which the Bishop was deprived for simony by Archbishop Tenison, in the reign of William III., and *Read v. the Bishop of Lincoln*,[2] in which the late Archbishop Benson had made a very careful examination of the Metropolitical jurisdiction of the Archbishop, to show that in these cases the citations were always to appear before the Archbishop or his Vicar-General. He further cited the forms observed at the Confirmations of Bishop Hampden and the present Bishop of Lincoln as proving that—

[1] 1 Ld. Raym., 447; 12 Mod. Rep., 237; Carth., 484.
[2] 14 P.D., 88, 148; [1891] P. 9; [1892] A.C. 644.

"The whole procedure takes judicial form; it takes it in a known court—namely, before his Grace or his Vicar-General; the Vicar-General sitting is treated as judge, and makes his decree as judge; he makes it in a proper ecclesiastical form, that of a definitive sentence in writing."

He then called attention to the curious anomaly that would result if the view of Confirmation contended for by the Crown lawyers was right:—

"The moment the decree of Confirmation is pronounced the Bishop becomes a Bishop complete, and has the spirituals and jurisdiction and so on committed to him, and from that very moment he could be tried by the Archbishop in this very court. It is a very curious thing that the Archbishop, in order to try him for heresy, must first make him a Bishop, and then try him and depose him, which would be an absurdity. Why should he not do it at the earliest suggestion, assuming that the statute admits it? Look at the curious result that would follow. While he is a Bishop-elect—a sort of embryo Bishop—this matter cannot be inquired into; but directly he is confirmed he can be tried, and deposed if he is found guilty."

Turning to a consideration of the statute 25 Henry VIII., c. 20, he asked their lordships to remember two things—(1) That this statute was one of a group carrying out a fixed policy; (2) that the whole of these statutes were repealed by Philip and Mary, and revived in a bundle, so to speak, by Elizabeth. Consequently, they must be looked at together and treated as throwing light upon one another. Another point that he wished to emphasise was that the policy of Henry VIII. was to cut the Church adrift from Rome. The whole of his statutes were aimed at that one policy—to free the Church entirely from the Bishop of Rome, and to make it self-contained in his realm. Again, it would have been extremely ill-advised on his part as a matter of policy to let a notion get abroad that his Bishops were Bishops who had not been submitted for ecclesiastical approval. His policy, therefore, was to do as little as possible by way of changing the previous state of things. He submitted that the object of the statute was simply to prevent the Archbishop from suing out Bulls from Rome.

Then as to the penalties of *praemunire*, that must mean " without lawful excuse." The Dean and Chapter would not incur a *praemunire* if the man mentioned in the King's Letters Missive were dead or under age. In the case of the Archbishop, the circumstances in which he should incur *praemunire* were carefully limited. If the King nominated a man under thirty years of age, was the Archbishop bound to confirm and consecrate? He submitted not, because he would be breaking another statute by doing so. If the Bishop-elect at Consecration refused to answer, or gave evasive answers to, the questions put to him in the Ordinal, was the Archbishop to go on with the Consecration? Would he incur a *praemunire* then? Surely not. He asked their lordships to draw the conclusion that the Act was not absolute, but meant that those whose duty it was to perform these acts should be guilty of the offence of *praemunire* if they neglected to do what was required of them without lawful excuse.

He then showed by reference to *Johnson's Dictionary* and the *Century Dictionary* that the word " confirm " implied mental approval, or some mental act beyond the mere putting a seal to it, or acting merely as a sort of conduit-pipe. It could not have been the intention of the Act of Parliament that the court should confirm merely as a sort of conduit-pipe. Even in ordinary everyday English the word "confirm" had never excluded mental approval or verification or inquiry, but had left the person to confirm an option. Still less could this be said of an ecclesiastical term used in an ecclesiastical Act with reference to ecclesiastical subject-matter and in collocation with other ecclesiastical terms. That Confirmation had been a judicial act was abundantly clear from the canonists. Ecclesiastical law in this country depended largely upon tradition. Down to a comparatively late period there were no reports, and they could only ascertain what the law was by seeing what forms and proceedings had in fact been applied. Directly the Act was passed these forms were adopted, and he asked their lordships to draw the inference that the Act was understood at the time of its passing by those who had to frame a course of procedure under it to require these things to be done. There had been a uniform and unbroken procedure. In the olden days, when the courts, particularly the ecclesiastical courts, proceeded according to a strict process, those processes and those laws were embodied and encrusted in a form which the courts used, and it was from that that they must infer the law. If he was right in his contention as to the meaning of the word "confirm," then these forms were practically conclusive. Were their lordships to throw over the forms and practice of 300 years upon a suggestion that they are a mere fiction? He submitted not. *Mr. Danckwerts* then cited a number of cases in which it had been laid down by the House of Lords that, where the language of a statute was doubtful, *contemporanea expositio*—*i.e.*, evidence as to the way in which the statute was understood at the time it was passed—must be called in to interpret. Here, he submitted, they had from the moment the statute was passed the adoption of the procedure which was used in the

Canon Law. They knew that the Canon Law was not a mere form, but a reality, and that under it objection could be taken to the election, the form of the election, and the person elected. It was established that a Confirmation to which opposers were not cited was void by the Canon Law. Unless their lordships were prepared to say that these proceedings, gone through, as he submitted, in a judicial tribunal, were idle shams, they were bound to say that opposers could be heard. There was not a trace that they were idle shams, but everything pointed to an opposite conclusion. He further submitted that at the recent Confirmation ceremony Mr. Cripps had no power to dispense with the second citation of opposers. According to the canon law, that alone was enough to render the Confirmation void. The Confirmation had been held without hearing the opponents, and was void and without jurisdiction, because it could not be held against the natural justice of hearing the parties who were entitled to be heard.

THE ATTORNEY-GENERAL'S REPLY.

Mr. Morton Smith having very briefly addressed the court upon the irregularity of the proceedings at the Church House, the *Attorney-General* then rose to reply. The *Lord Chief Justice* at once intimated that their lordships did not want a general reply, but would be glad to have their attention called to any special matter which they ought to have before them. The *Attorney-General* first pointed out that if the contention put forward by the other side were correct, the Crown would actually be in a worse position as regards presentation to bishoprics than the patron of an ordinary living, who, if his presentee were rejected, had his remedy by *quare impedit*, and now under the Benefices Act. That of itself was enough to destroy the argument, which proved too much. On the point of the Vicar-General's jurisdiction he then showed from Oughton's *Ordo Judiciorum* and a curious manuscript volume of forms and precedents, dating back to 1597, in the possession of Mr. Dibdin (which was said to have lain for 200 years at the Moravian Chapel in Fetter-lane, and to have been advertised for sale as an old copy of the Thirty-nine Articles), that as far back as 1597 the practice had prevailed of appointing the same person Judge of the Court of Audience and Vicar-General. He could not trace the history of the office further back than the date mentioned, which was within a century of the passing of the statute. He protested against the statement put forward by counsel for the respondents that it followed from the argument for the Crown that the ceremony of Consecration was a mere form, and said that the passages cited from Justinian, Lancelottus, Van Espen, the *Decretum Gratiani*, and the Decretals of Gregory IX. would not bear the construction which had been put upon them. As to the arguments of Mr. Haldane that the statute of Henry VIII. restored the normal state of things, and of Mr. Bramwell Davis that there had been a continuous practice down to the time of the statute, it was admitted that there had been a break from 1316 onwards. If they were dealing with geological periods, a break of more than 200 years would be quite unimportant; but in dealing with the comparatively modern history of this country, the argument scarcely held good. He relied strongly on the canon of construction laid down in *Ridsdale* v. *Clifton*[1]:—

"Were the language of the statute obscure, instead of

---

[1] 2 P. D. at p. 331, quoting judgment of Lord Campbell in *Gorham* v. *Bishop of Exeter*, 15 Q.B. at pp. 73, 74.

being clear, we should not be justified in differing from the construction put upon it by contemporaneous and long-continued usage. There would be no safety for property or liberty if it could be successfully contended that all lawyers and statesmen have been mistaken for centuries as to the true meaning of an old Act of Parliament."

The *Attorney-General* then dealt with certain points which had been raised in connection with the case of *Evans* v. *Ascuithe*,[1] decided in 1629, and the writs under the statute 3 Henry V. in Rymer's *Foedera*, and submitted that they in no way helped the contention against the Crown. As to Suffragan-Bishops, Mr. Danckwerts had fallen into an amusing error when he said that he himself had settled the first form under the statute 26 Henry VIII., c. 14. If so, his friend must be a good deal older than he thought, because he had himself referred to certainly fourteen cases in the sixteenth century, though it was true that a gap existed between the reign of Elizabeth and the revival of the statute in modern times.

The arguments concluded at three o'clock, their lordships reserving judgment.

[The judgments will be found printed in *Rex. v. Archbishop of Canterbury*, [1902] 2 K.B., pp. 537–573, and in the *Times* of February 11, 1902].

[1] W. Jones, 158; Palm. 457.

IN DEFENCE OF THE CHURCH

From a Legal Standpoint

[These two articles, together with the Summary of judgments relating to the Ornaments of the Church and the Minister which follows, first appeared in a "Westminster Popular," entitled "The Crisis in the Church, a full Statement of the Case," published by the *Westminster Gazette* in October, 1899. They are here reprinted by the permission of the Proprietor and Editor of that journal, to whom my thanks are due.—C. Y. S.]

CHAPTER I

THE CHURCH AND PARLIAMENT

I HAVE been asked to state as briefly as possible what is the nature of the objection taken by High Churchmen to two propositions, which are constantly and confidently put forward as political axioms admitting of no dispute in discussing the position of an Established Church. It is said (1) that Parliament alone is the supreme legislative authority for the Church on all matters of doctrine and discipline; (2) that all questions involving the decision of points of doctrine and ritual are rightly submitted in the last resort to a lay tribunal deriving its authority from Parliament only. Both these propositions are strenuously denied by High Churchmen, Ritualist and Moderate alike, and it becomes a matter of importance to ascertain what are the grounds of their objection. The denial of the first proposition rests upon the belief that the assent of the clergy in their Convocations to all legislative Acts affecting the Church is constitutionally necessary to the validity of such Acts, and that without such assent the Church is not legally bound by them. The Convocations it is said, representing the clergy, gave in past times the assent of one part of the body politic, while Parliament, which was simply the laity of the Church in its legislative capacity, gave the assent of the other. The precise Constitutional position of the Convocations in pre-Reformation times is not easy to determine. They met by the King's writ to vote subsidies to the Crown, a right which they retained until it was tacitly dropped in 1664, and as Provincial Synods they had power to pass canons which were enforceable in the Ecclesiastical Courts. By the Submission of the Clergy in 1533 they acknowledged the King as "Supreme Head of the Church on earth, so far as the law of Christ allows," and bound themselves not to issue any new canons without the King's Royal Assent and Licence, a restriction which has never been relaxed. This was confirmed by statute in the following year. There is apparently no ground for saying that legislative proposals affecting the Church intended to be laid before Parliament were at any time necessarily submitted to Convocation; but there is ample evidence to show that at critical periods of the Church's history, when sweeping changes in doctrine and discipline were contemplated, such matters were generally, though not invariably, referred to Convocation for consideration and approval before any attempt was made to give them the force of statute-law. Thus the Submission of the Clergy, however reluctantly conceded by Convocation, became the basis of the Statute which fixed the system of ecclesiastical appeals in England. The Statute of the Six Articles,[1] as the preamble recites, was passed after the King "had caused his most High Court of Parliament to be summoned; and also a Synod and Convocation of all the Archbishops and Bishops and other learned men of the Clergy of his Realm . . . . in which

---

[1] 31 Henry VIII., c. 14.

Parliament and Convocation there were certain Articles set forth .... as well by the assent of the Lords Spiritual and Temporal, and other learned men of his clergy in their Convocations, and by the consent of the Commons in this present Parliament assembled," &c. Even the Act authorising "the King's Grace to be Supreme Head," 26 Henry VIII., c. 1, now repealed, in which the assertion of the King's Supremacy rose, perhaps, to its highest point, begins by reciting the recognition of the Supreme Headship "by the clergy of this realm in their Convocations." The records of the Convocation of the Southern Province unfortunately perished in the Great Fire of London of 1666, and it is only by side lights and fragmentary excerpts by historians who had access to them before the Fire that the course of events can be conjectured with any degree of accuracy. The Houses, when not engaged in taxation, appear to have been largely occupied with questions of heresy and other matters of purely spiritual cognisance. It has been much debated whether the First and Second Prayer-books of Edward VI., which were drawn up by a committee of Bishops and divines, were ever submitted to Convocation. Lathbury, in his "History of Convocation,"[1] following some older authorities, asserts positively that they were; but a recent historian of the period, Dom Gasquet, in his *Edward VI. and the Book of Common Prayer*,[2] gives very good reasons for thinking that they were not. It seems certain at any rate that Convocation was not consulted as to the passing of either of the Acts of Uniformity, which gave to the Edwardian Prayer-books the force of law. Convocation appears to have declared in favour of communion in both kinds before the Order of Communion was put forth in 1548, and to have ratified and confirmed Cranmer's Forty-Two

[1] 1842, p. 142.   [2] Chap. X.

Articles of Religion in 1552.[1] The Elizabethan Act of Uniformity, as the late Archbishop Temple reminded us at the Lambeth Hearing on Incense and Processional Lights in 1899, was passed without the assent of Convocation, owing probably to the troubled state of the times, and the fact that of the Bench of Bishops half were dead, and the remainder for the most part disaffected. The Thirty-nine Articles, as the Prayer-book tells us, were " agreed upon by the Archbishops and Bishops of both provinces, and the whole Clergy in the Convocation holden at London in the year 1562," were confirmed by them in 1571, and received statutory authority in the same year. The Declaration prefixed to the Articles in our present Prayer-book, authorised by Charles I. and believed to have been the work of Laud, states that " We are Supreme Governor of the Church of England, and if any difference arise about the external Policy, concerning the Injunctions, Canons, and other Constitutions whatsoever thereto belonging, the Clergy in their Convocation is to order and settle them, having first obtained leave under Our Broad Seal so to do; and We approving their said Ordinances and Constitutions etc. . . ." The Canons of 1603, which are binding on the clergy at the present day, were drawn up by the Convocation of Canterbury, with the King's licence, subsequently agreed to by the Convocation of York, and published by the Royal authority under the Great Seal of England. They were never confirmed by Parliament, and hence have been held by the Courts [2] not to be binding on the laity, a decision which lends some colour to the contention that in matters of religion regulations intended to bind the whole nation must receive the assent of both clergy and laity,

---

[1] Lathbury, *History of Convocation*, pp. 141, 144.

[2] *Middleton* v. *Croft*, 2 Stra. 1056; 2 Atk. 640, Judgment of Lord Hardwicke (1737).

each in their proper assembly. In 1662 was passed the last Act of Uniformity, the preamble to which recites that "the Convocations of both the provinces of Canterbury and York being by his Majesty called and assembled and now sitting, his Majesty has been pleased to authorise and require the presidents of the said Convocations and other the Bishops and clergy of the same to review the said Book of Common Prayer, &c., and that after mature consideration they should make such additions and alterations . . . . as to them should seem meet and convenient, and present the same to his Majesty in writing for his further allowance or confirmation. . . . All which his Majesty having duly considered both fully approved and allowed the same, and recommended to this present Parliament that the said Book of Common Prayer, &c., with the alterations and additions which have been so made, and presented to his Majesty by the said Convocations, be the book which shall be appointed to be used, &c. . . ."

In 1689 a Commission was appointed by William and Mary to draw up a scheme for a revision of the liturgy in such a sense that Dissenters could conscientiously accept it, which made shipwreck on the opposition of the Lower House of Convocation. The important facts, as given by Lathbury,[1] are thus stated : "Many there were, especially the Dissenters, who wished to settle all matters in Parliament, but the House of Commons were of opinion that the Convocation was the proper place for the consideration of ecclesiastical affairs. . . . On May 24th, 1689, the Act of Toleration received the Royal assent. Still, many Dissenters wished for a comprehension with the Church. A Bill on the subject had passed the House of Lords ; but on its reaching the Commons they considered that the question was more suitable for a Convocation. The Lords,

[1] *History of Convocation*, p. 265.

therefore, concurred in an address to the Throne to that effect."

A few authorities may here be cited. Sir Matthew Hale (temp. Car. II.), in his unfinished treatise, *Touching the Rights of the Crown*,[1] while asserting the power of the King " by assent of Parliament to make laws in matters ecclesiastical," speaks of the " courteous usage of this Kingdom," which " did in former times indulge a kind of legislative power to the Convocation of the clergy."

Bishop Atterbury, in his *Rights, Powers, and Privileges of an English Convocation Stated and Vindicated*, (1701),[2] in answer to Archbishop Wake's *The Authority of Christian Princes over their Ecclesiastical Synods* (1697), quotes the following writers:—

Sir Robert Cotton, in his *Posthuma*, p. 215, has these words: "If any shall object, that many laws, in Henry the Eighth's time, had first the ground in Parliament, it is manifested, by the dates of their Acts in Convocation, that they all had in that place their first original."

Fuller, at p. 188 of his *Church History*, Sixteenth Century, speaks as follows: " Upon serious examination it will appear, that there was nothing done in the Reformation of Religion, save what was acted by the Clergy in their Convocations, or grounded on some Act of theirs precedent to it, with the advice, counsel, and consent of the Bishops and most eminent Church-men; confirmed upon the *Post-fact*, and not otherwise, by the civil sanction; according to the usage of the best and purest times of Christianity."

" To which " (continues Bishop Atterbury[3]), " I shall add the testimony of one who must be allowed a good

---

[1] Privately printed by Mr. (now Sir) Lewis T. Dibdin from a MS. in the possession of the Benchers of Lincoln's Inn, 1884.

[2] P. 179.   [3] P. 180.

witness in this case, my Lord of Sarum (Burnet): He assures the Bishop of Meaux (Bossuet) in the answer he made to his *Variations,* 'that our Parliaments and Princes have not meddled in matters of Religion any other way, but that they have given the civil sanction to the propositions made by the Church: and this is that which Christian Princes do in all places.'"

Atterbury concludes: "And in 1604, I find a Puritan writer making this challenge: 'Let them, if they can, show any one instance of any change or alteration, either from religion to superstition, or from superstition to religion, to have been made in Parliament, unless the same, freely and at large, have been first agreed upon in their Synods and Convocations.' Which," he adds, "is no otherwise considerable, I own, than as it comes from the pen of an adversary."

Archbishop Wake himself, in the treatise above mentioned, refers to the religious settlement of 1662 as having been carried out in the "most solemn, the most undoubtedly authoritative way of transacting such matters, viz., when the King, designing any constitution of a more than ordinary concern to the Church or realm, does for the more prudent establishment of it (1) by a select committee prepare what he thinks needful to propose to the Convocation concerning it; then (2) has it examined and concluded there; and (3) having reviewed it with his Privy Council and his learned counsel in the law, (4) finally refers it to his two Houses of Parliament, where, being also consented to and approved of, he (5) finally himself subscribes to it, and makes it a part of the Statute Law of the realm."[1]

---

[1] *Authority of Christian Princes over their Ecclesiastical Synods,* 1697, Chapter IV., p. 257, quoted in Montagu Burrows' *Parliament and the Church of England,* at p. 83.

Professor Montagu Burrows in his *Parliament and the Church of England* (1875), p. 123, summing up an inquiry into the relations of Church and State from an opposite standpoint to that which is here assumed, claims to have proved " that, since the Reformation was effected, as it has never been admitted that the clergy, with or without the Sovereign, have any exclusive right to deal with the affairs of the Church, so *Parliament has not entertained any questions of doctrine or ceremony without reference to the clergy.* It has simply asserted its claim to protect what had been established by general consent at the Reformation." High Churchmen ask for no more than is here conceded, but they will be content with no less.

Enough, it is submitted, has been said to show that the claim that Parliament is the sole supreme legislative authority for the Church is a claim which cannot be supported by history. Parliament itself, when it was exclusively composed of Churchmen, disclaimed, as we have seen, any such right. Still less is the proposition true of a Parliament composed, as is that of the present day, of men of all religions and none. It is beyond question that at most crucial periods of the nation's religious history, even under the despotic Tudors and arbitrary Stuarts, the clergy in their Convocations were freely consulted and deferred to before measures of vital importance were taken in hand. The claim put forward on behalf of Parliament is, in fact, a modern one, which has grown to its present strength and volume owing to circumstances which are easily explained. In 1717, after the accession of the House of Hanover, Convocation, which had become a prey to political and theological wrangles, was virtually suppressed, and lay forgotten in the lumber-room of the Constitution for one hundred and thirty-five years.

The weakening of the High Church Tories by their attachment to the House of Stuart, and by the Non-Juring schism, the long ascendancy of the Whigs, the appointment of Erastian and Latitudinarian Bishops by the Government, the consequent apathy and depression of the Church, the religious deadness of the Eighteenth Century, the waning power of the Crown, which down to the time of Queen Anne had stood in a personal relationship to the Church, the ever-increasing power of the House of Commons, the growing political importance of the Dissenters, and, lastly, the removal of all religious tests and disabilities, combined to place the Church in the position in which we now find her. The traditional ecclesiastical polity has disappeared, the old constitutional courtesies are out of date, the rights of the Church are forgotten or denied altogether. Side by side with this political atrophy, the Church meanwhile has grown in spiritual power and stature, with revived energies and exuberant activities. She has awakened to find herself bound hand and foot by the obsolete restraints of Tudor statutes on the one hand, and half-throttled by the chains of modern political restrictions on the other. Disestablishment is one way out of her difficulties; the Reform of Convocation and its restoration in some degree to its old position in the body politic is another.[1] The Convocations do not at present adequately represent the clergy, and the Houses of Laymen are at best but a makeshift and temporary vehicle for expressing the voice of the Church laity. Parliament and the Convocations can never, of course, again stand in the old intimate relationship to one another, since Parliament is co-extensive with the nation and the Church is not. But so long as the legislative sanction of

[1] This was written before the creation of that important and most hopeful body, The Representative Church Council.

Parliament is necessary to every, even the smallest, change in the constitution of the Church, there would seem to be nothing unreasonable or unworkable in a scheme whereby the reformed Convocations, adequately representative of clergy and laity alike, should be consulted by Parliament as of old upon every matter affecting her life and work. In place of friction and thinly-veiled or undisguised hostility, we might yet live to see two self-respecting and autonomous assemblies, each within its proper sphere, working harmoniously side by side for the common weal in Church and State.

CHAPTER II.

THE CHURCH AND THE PRIVY COUNCIL.

IT remains to consider the objection of High Churchmen to the appellate jurisdiction of the Privy Council over the doctrine and ritual of the Church, and to explain why they regard the subordination of the Church to a purely secular tribunal as contrary to the Reformation Settlement. It is assumed by the average Englishman that this jurisdiction necessarily flows from the principle of the Royal Supremacy, though few have any clear idea as to what, historically and constitutionally, this principle means. Whatever it may have meant in the mouths of the Tudors, it is argued, not without some show of reason, that, viewed in the light of the constitutional development, which has so deeply affected the life of the nation in its secular aspect, it means *now* the supremacy of the laity expressed through Parliament, and through the Executive Government and the judicial system which Parliament has set up. As the Church has within recent years

POINTS OF CHURCH LAW

been referred with crushing force to a statute of Elizabeth as barring the way to all modern ritual developments,[1] it seems only fair to give her the benefit of those statutes which fixed her constitutional status under Henry VIII. We shall at least be enabled to see what Henry and his Parliament, who certainly did not err on the side of tenderness to the clergy, held to be the rightful place of the Church in the body politic. The first statute bearing on the subject is the Act for the Restraint of Appeals, 24 Henry VIII., c. 12, one of the foundation statutes of the Reformation, the preamble to which runs as follows:

" Where by divers sundry old authentick Histories and Chronicles, it is manifestly declared and expressed, that this Realm of England is an Empire, and so hath been accepted in the World, governed by one supreme Head and King . . . unto whom a Body politick, compact of all sorts and degrees of people, divided in terms and by names of Spiritualty and Temporalty, been (*sic*) bounden and owen to bear, next to God, a natural and humble obedience; he being also institute and furnished by the Goodness and Sufferance of Almighty God, with plenary, whole, and entire Power, Preeminence, Authority, Prerogative, and Jurisdiction, to render and yield justice, and final determination to all manner of folk, resiants, or subjects within this his realm, in all causes, matters, debates, and contentions, happening to occur, insurge, or begin within the limits thereof, without restraint, or provocation [*i.e.*, appeal] to any foreign Princes or Potentates of the World ; the Body Spiritual whereof having power, when any cause of the Law Divine happened to come in question, or of Spiritual Learning, then it was declared, interpreted, and shewed by that part of the said Body

---

[1] Archbishops' Hearing on Incense and Processional Lights. July 31, 1899.

politick, called the Spiritualty, now being usually called the English Church, which always hath been reputed, and also found of that sort, that both for knowledge, integrity, and sufficiency of number, it hath been always thought, and is also at this hour, sufficient and meet of itself, without the intermeddling of any exterior person or persons, to declare and determine all such doubts, and to administer all such offices and duties, as to their rooms spiritual doth appertain, . . . and the Laws temporal, for trial of property, of lands and goods, . . . was and yet is administered, adjudged, and executed by sundry judges and ministers of the other part of the Body politick, called the Temporalty; and both their authorities and jurisdictions do conjoin together in the due administration of justice, the one to help the other."

This preamble, next to the famous words in Magna Charta, *Ecclesia Anglicana libera sit*, is the charter on which the spiritual independence of the Church of England rests. It asserts (1) that there is a body politic divided into Spiritualty and Temporalty; (2) that the King is the head of this body, and that his duty is to "render and yield justice and final determination to all manner of folk"; (3) that the Spiritualty has power to declare and interpret all causes of the Law Divine and spiritual learning; (4) that it has always been "meet and sufficient of itself without the intermeddling of any exterior person" (a reference, doubtless, to the claims of the Pope), "to declare and determine all such doubts." (5) That the laws temporal are administered by temporal judges representing the Temporalty, and (6) that these two co-ordinate and independent jurisdictions are associated in the administration of justice, "the one to help the other." The independence of the Spiritualty is affirmed in the clearest terms, the function of the Crown being limited to the task of seeing that justice is done to all its subjects.

The language of Lord Coke in *Cawdrey's Case*, a suit in which the legality of deprivation by the Court of High Commission came into question (tem. Jac. I.), is very similar :[1]

" By the ancient laws of this realm this kingdom is an absolute empire and monarchy consisting of one head, which is the King, and of a body politic, compact and compounded of many, and almost infinite, several and yet well agreeing members : all which the law divideth into two several parts, that is to say, 'the clergy and the laity,' both of them next and immediately under God, subject and obedient to the head : also the Kingly head of this politic body is instituted and furnished with plenary and entire power, prerogative, and jurisdiction, to render justice and right to every part and member of this body, of what estate, degree, or calling soever in all causes ecclesiastical or temporal, otherwise he should not be head of the whole body. And as in temporal causes, the King, by the mouth of the Judges in his Courts of Justice doth judge and determine the same by the temporal laws of England : so in causes ecclesiastical and spiritual, as namely blasphemy, apostacy from Christianity, heresies, schisms . . . celebration of Divine Service . . . appeals in ecclesiastical causes, commutation of penance, and others (the connusance whereof belongs not to the common laws of England) the same are to be determined and decided by ecclesiastical Judges, according to the King's ecclesiastical laws of this realm," which he explains to mean such ecclesiastical laws derived *ab extra*, *i.e.*, the canons and constitutions of the Church, " as were proved, approved, and allowed here by and with a general consent."

[1] Co. Rep. Part V. p. 8.

It is not denied that the claims of the Tudors rose a good deal higher than the preamble to 24 Henry VIII., c. 12, under what Professor Montagu Burrows calls the "Dictatorship, temporarily accepted as a necessity, then suffered under protest or actively opposed."[1] Henry VIII., in the latter years of his reign, attributed to himself powers that were almost Godlike in dealing with the Church. Thus 26 Henry VIII., c. 1, a statute repealed by Philip and Mary and never revived, gave to the King "full power and authority . . . to visit, repress, redress, reform, order, correct, restrain, and amend all such *errors*, *heresies*, abuses, offences, contempts, and enormities, whatsoever they be, which by any manner *Spiritual authority* or jurisdiction ought or may be lawfully reformed, redressed, &c., most to the pleasure of Almighty God, the increase of virtue in Christ's religion, and for the conservation of the peace, unity, and tranquillity of this Realm." Again in 37 Henry VIII., c. 17,[2] "A Bill that Doctors of Civil Law being married may exercise ecclesiastical jurisdiction," Henry's Parliament, in a peculiarly servile address to the King, asserts "that where your most Royal Majesty is and hath always justly been, by the Word of God, Supreme Head in Earth of the Church of England, and hath full power and authority to correct, punish, and repress all manner of *heresies*, *errors*, vices, sins, abuses, idolatries, hypocrisies, and superstitions, sprung and growing within the same, and to *exercise all other manner of jurisdictions, commonly called ecclesiastical jurisdiction*, &c. . . ." Even Elizabeth, who modestly disclaimed the title of "Supreme Head" in favour of that of "Supreme Governor" of the Church, suffered her Parliament to address her in the first year of her reign

---

[1] *Parliament and the Church of England* (1875), p. 124.
[2] Repealed by S.L.R. Act, 1863, 26 and 27 Vict., c. 125.

in language, which still stands in the Statute-book, as follows :

"And that it may likewise please your Highness, that it may be established and enacted by the authority aforesaid, that such jurisdictions, privileges, superiorities, and pre-eminences *spiritual and ecclesiastical, as by any spiritual or ecclesiastical power or authority hath heretofore been, or may lawfully be exercised or used for the visitation of the ecclesiastical state* and persons, and for reformation, order and correction of the same, and of all manner of *errors, heresies*, schisms, abuses, offences, contempts and enormities, shall for ever by authority of this present Parliament be united and annexed to the Imperial Crown of this Realm." (1 Eliz., c. 1, s. 17.)[1]

The times, it must be remembered, were exceptional; England was locked in the death-grapple with the power of the Papacy, resistance to which rather than a desire to enslave the Church was the governing motive of the legislation of the day. The section of the Act of Elizabeth must be read in connection with the famous "High Commission section," afterwards repealed, which immediately follows, and under which Elizabeth and the first two Stuarts worked their obnoxious Court.

The statute of 24 Henry VIII., c. 12, which prohibited appeals to Rome, established a complete system of ecclesiastical appeals within the realm. "Causes testamentary, causes of matrimony and divorce, right of tithes, oblations and obventions," in which appeals had lain to the See of Rome, were thenceforward to be "heard, examined, dis-

---

[1] Bishop Stubbs describes this section as "restoring to the Crown in modified form the *visitatorial and corrective* authority recognised by 26 Henry VIII., c. i., as belonging to the Supremacy, but not containing the indefinite claims annexed to the title by that Act." (Eccl. Courts Commission, Historical Appendix (1), p. 44.)

cussed, clearly, finally, and definitively adjudged and determined within the King's jurisdiction and authority, and not elsewhere, in the Courts spiritual and temporal of the same." Appeals were to go from the inferior ecclesiastical Courts to the Archbishop of the province, by whom they were to be "definitively and finally determined"; while in any matter or contention touching the King (such as Queen Katherine's divorce then pending), the appeal was to be to the "spiritual Prelates and other Abbots and Priors" of the Upper House of Convocation, whose sentence was to be final.

The system of appeals thus established was tentative and experimental, and in the following year, when the Act of the Submission of the Clergy, 25 Henry VIII., c. 19, was passed, the matter was again dealt with. Section 4[1] of that Act runs as follows:

"And for lack of justice at or in any the Courts of the Archbishops of this realm, or in any the King's dominions, it shall be lawful to the parties grieved to appeal to the King's Majesty in the King's Court of Chancery; and that upon every such appeal, a Commission shall be directed under the Great Seal to such persons as shall be named by the King's Highness, his heirs or successors, like as in case of appeal from the Admiral's Court, to hear and definitively determine such appeals, and the causes concerning the same. Which Commissioners, so by the King's Highness, his heirs or successors, to be named or appointed, shall have full power and authority to hear and definitively determine every such appeal, with the causes and all circumstances concerning the same; and that such judgment and sentence, as the said Commissioners shall make and decree, in and upon any such appeal, shall be good and effectual, and also definitive; and no further

---

[1] Repealed by 2 and 3 Will. IV., c. 92, s. 1.

appeals to be had or made from the said Commissioners for the same."

This section is the foundation-stone on which has been built up the whole fabric of the appellate jurisdiction of the Crown in causes ecclesiastical. Its scope and meaning have long been the subject of controversy. On the one hand, it is claimed by High Churchmen that the section does no more than assert the right and duty of the Crown to see that no wrong goes unredressed. The King is the fountain of justice—the natural protector of all his subjects, and if any man suffer wrong in the highest ecclesiastical Court, the King will see him righted. On the other hand, it is asserted that the section covers all those matters of doctrine and ritual on which the Privy Council so freely adjudicated during the reign of Queen Victoria. The words "lack of justice" and "parties grieved," and the way in which the Act was worked for three hundred years, seem to favour the former view, and point to the conclusion that the powers now exercised by the Crown through the Judicial Committee of the Privy Council are the result rather of constitutional changes and political exigencies than the logical outcome of the statute itself. The old High Court of Delegates was not a permanent Court. Upon every appeal the Lord Chancellor of the day issued a commission to certain Bishops, Judges, and Doctors of the Civil Law, who formed the Court to try the particular cause in hand. There was no fixed rule by which the Commissioners were appointed, and after 1751 the Bishops dropped out altogether. Their proceedings were dilatory and expensive, and gave so little satisfaction to suitors that in 1832 a Royal Commission readily reported in favour of abolishing their jurisdiction and transferring ecclesiastical appeals to the Privy Council, the judicial functions of which were then about to undergo reorganisation. A peculiarity of the Delegates' procedure was that they upheld or reversed the decision of the Spiritual Court below, without giving any reasons for their ruling. They merely answered Ay or No, for or against the "party grieved." This practice, while it constituted a valuable safeguard against the formation of a possibly mistaken body of ecclesiastical precedents, was felt as a serious hardship by suitors, who had no means of knowing on what grounds their appeals had been rejected : and the adoption by the Privy Council, after the legislative changes of William the Fourth's reign, of the practice of delivering one reasoned judgment on behalf of the whole Committee was thought to be a great improvement. But the Church has paid a heavy price for the change. Instead of the Judicial Committee advising his Majesty as to the rights or wrongs of the particular "party grieved," their judgments have come to be regarded as forming a fixed body of ecclesiastical law, without even the safeguard of permission to dissentient members of the Court to declare the fact, much less the grounds, of their dissent. A reform of the practice of the Court in this respect,[1] and a return to the old system of treating each decision as applicable only to the particular case in hand, find favour with some eminent authorities as one way out of the Church's present difficulties.

There has been much discussion on the subject-matter of the appeals which came before the Delegates, and especially as to whether they ever adjudicated upon matters of doctrine. It is clear that in law whatever appeals went

[1] The Ecclesiastical Courts Commission, 1883, p. 58, reported thus : "The judges shall not be bound to state reasons for their decision, but if they do so, each judge shall deliver his judgment separately as in the Supreme Court of Judicature and the House of Lords."

POINTS OF CHURCH LAW 107

to the Pope before the Reformation passed by 24 Henry VIII., c. 12, to the Archbishop as judge in the last resort, thence by 25 Henry VIII., c. 19, "for lack of justice" to the Delegates representing the King in Chancery, and finally by the legislation of William IV. to the King in Council. If the Pope could entertain appeals in matters of doctrine, it is argued, so can the Privy Council. The authorities are not at one on this point. Bishop Stubbs, in his Historical Appendix to the Report of the Ecclesiastical Courts Commission, 1883, concludes that "there was no custom of appealing on such points to the Pope," that as in the Statute of Henry "no express mention is made of appeals on questions of doctrine and ritual," no new right of appeal was given to the Delegates where it had not before existed, and that "the maintenance of the existing jurisdiction of the Judicial Committee of the Privy Council, as a final tribunal of appeal in matters of doctrine and ritual, is not to be regarded as an essential part, or necessary historical consequence, of the Reformation Settlement."[1] Lord Halifax believes that appeals to Rome were limited to the "causes testamentary, causes of matrimony and divorces, right of tithes, oblations, and obventions," mentioned in 24 Henry VIII., c. 12. On the other side, the late Professor Maitland[2] argues on what appear to be conclusive grounds, that appeals in matters of doctrine did go to the Pope, and the Dean of the Arches, Sir Lewis Dibdin, is understood to be of the same opinion. The evidence as to the actual practice of the Delegates on this point is somewhat obscure. So long as the Court of High Commission lasted, cases of heresy were dealt with by that Court, and the jurisdiction of the Delegates was practically superseded.

[1] P. 51.
[2] Canon Law in the Church of England (1898).

The records of their proceedings are defective during a long period; but of the seven causes involving questions of doctrine known to have come before them, "the proceedings" (says Bishop Stubbs) "were discontinued in three cases before a decision was arrived at: in one the sentence of the Court below was confirmed; in two it was varied, but not so as to protect the appellant; in one, in which the original promoter was the appellant, the appeal was renounced."[1] This seems a rather slender basis of fact on which to build up a theory of a complete system of appellate jurisdiction in questions of faith and ritual as residing in the Delegates. It must be borne in mind that down to 1857 the Spiritual Courts had exclusive connusance of causes testamentary and matrimonial, and the time of the Delegates was largely occupied with appeals on matters of this nature.

Then came the legislation of the first reformed Parliament, which swept away the Delegates, and annexed their jurisdiction to the Privy Council. It was the moment of calm before the storm. The Oxford Movement was not yet launched, no one at that time anticipated an outbreak of ritual and doctrinal controversies, and the measure, which had the approval of the highest Church authorities, slipped easily through.[2] Lord Brougham, the author of the Bill, stated in the House of Lords in 1850, in the hubbub which followed the delivery of the Gorham judgment, that the prospects of such appeals coming before the new tribunal had never so much as crossed his mind. The Privy Council (in the words of Bishop Stubbs) appears to have acquired its present position in the hierarchy of ecclesiastical appeals "by no conscious act of the Legisla-

[1] P. 51.
[2] Keble is said to have protested against it.

ture, and by no conscious acquiescence of the Church, but rather by a series of overlookings and takings for granted, by the assumption of successive generations of lawyers and the laches or want of foresight on the part of the clergy."[1] As in the case of the legislative, so with regard to the judicial, functions of the Spiritualty, it is claimed that there has been a gradual departure from the spirit of the Reformation Settlement—call it constitutional development, or what you will—and that the present state of things is the result of an unconscious or half-conscious usurpation and aggression, the State blindly encroaching, and the clergy blindly acquiescing, until the ancient constitutional landmarks have been obliterated altogether.

The Body Spiritual, says the statute of Henry VIII., had power, when any cause of the Law Divine happened to come in question, or of spiritual learning, to declare and interpret such questions, and the Spiritualty, "now being commonly called the English Church," was "of that sort, both for knowledge, integrity, and sufficiency of number," that it had always been thought "sufficient and meet of itself to declare and determine all such doubts, and to administer all such offices and duties, as to their rooms spiritual doth appertain." Is the Spiritualty of the present day one whit behind the Spiritualty of 1533 in its meetness and sufficiency for these duties? Is there anything outrageous or offensive to a reasonable lay mind in the proposed resumption by the Spiritualty of powers and duties thus clearly recognised by the Legislature? The proposal adopted by the Lower House of Canterbury Convocation, in discussing the late Archbishop Benson's Ecclesiastical Procedure Bill, of a clause whereby the opinion of the Episcopate, solemnly delivered after formal reference to that body, on a point

[1] Ecclesiastical Courts Commission, Historical Appendix (1), p. 51.

of doctrine or ritual, should be binding on the Privy Council in doing justice to a "party grieved" would, it is contended, be simply a return to ancient theory. This proposal was actually embodied in a Bill introduced into the House of Lords by Bishop Blomfield in 1850. Similar recommendations have found a place in the Report of the Ecclesiastical Courts Commission, 1883, p. 58, and in the Report of the Royal Commission on Ecclesiastical Discipline, 1906, pp. 69, 77, and 78. Had such a provision been in existence at the time of the Gorham case, when "certain causes of the Law Divine and of spiritual learning" came into question, the Judicial Committee, to which it fell to determine whether Mr. Gorham had been rightly or wrongly denied institution to his benefice by the Bishop of Exeter, would have referred certain questions to the whole body of Bishops to ascertain what was the doctrine of the Church of England on these points, and on receipt of the answer would have applied their minds, with or without the assistance of theological assessors, to the question whether, in fact, Mr. Gorham had by his teaching contravened that doctrine. Even this would have been a delicate matter to confide to the purely legal mind, untrained in theology. Such mixed questions of temporal right and spiritual jurisdiction would be, under any system, extremely difficult to adjust. What is here contended for is that the point before the Privy Council was simply the point of Mr. Gorham's right to the temporalities of the benefice of Bramford Speke, his fitness for which was, or should have been, a matter for the determination of the Spiritualty. It is often said that the Privy Council merely interprets, and does not define, the doctrines of the Church; but in practice, as all lawyers know, you cannot interpret without defining, and in point of fact it is well known that the Privy Council has by its judgments, while narrowly restricting the limits of permissible *ritual*, enlarged the latitude of permissible *belief* to be required from the clergy of the Church of England. That this delicate and difficult task of interpretation should be entrusted to a lay tribunal, deriving its authority from Parliament alone rather than to the Spiritualty, whose proper function it has been by Parliament itself authoritatively declared to be, is not, it is contended, a legitimate deduction from the principles which have guided the English Reformation, but the contrary. If it be indeed the will of the nation that the Church should remain by law established, a return to the old paths by the concession to the Spiritualty of this right in some form or other is, in the view of High Churchmen, the only possible and tolerable condition of establishment.

NOTE ON THE AUTHORITY OF THE CANONS OF 1603.

The canons are binding on the clergy, but not on the laity. Lord Coke lays it down in Part XII. of his *Reports*:—

"A Convocation may make constitutions by which those of the Spiritualty shall be bound, for this, that they all, or by representation, or in person, are present, but not the Temporalty." (*Of Convocations*, 12 Co., p. 73 ; vol. VI. of ed. of 1826, p. 294.)

In the case of *Matthew* v. *Burdett*, in the King's Bench in 1703, it was said :—

"If the King and clergy make a canon, it binds the clergy *in re ecclesiastica*, but it does not bind laymen, they are not represented in Convocation ; their consent is neither asked nor given." (2 Salkeld's *Reports*, p. 412.)

In *Cox's case* (1700) the Lord Keeper Wright said :—
"The canons of a Convocation do not bind the laity without an Act of Parliament." (1 Peere Williams' *Reports*, p. 32.)

The question was considered at great length by Lord Hardwicke in the case of *Middleton* v. *Croft* (1737), 2 Strange's *Reports*, p. 1056 ; 2 Atkyns' *Reports*, p. 650. In his judgment he thus expresses himself :—

[The canons of 1603] "were made by the Bishops and clergy in Convocation assembled, by virtue of the King's writ, and confirmed by his Charter, under the Great Seal. The general opinion has been that these, having never been received or confirmed in Parliament, cannot bind the laity. . . . . It may be proper to settle it, and we are all of opinion that *proprio vigore* the canons of 1603 do not bind the laity ; I say *proprio vigore* because some of them are only declaratory of the ancient canon law. . . . The King's consent to a canon *in re ecclesiastica* makes it a law to bind the clergy, but not the laity ; and no one can say that the consent of the people is included in the Royal confirmation."

The Royal assent to these canons was given by James I. by Letters Patent dated September 6th, 1604 ; according to the statute 25 Henry VIII., c. 19, the Act for the Submission of the Clergy. (*Vide Rex* v. *Archbishop of York* (1795), 6 *Term Reports*, p. 490.) The consent of Parliament was neither asked nor given.

The subject will be found fully and learnedly discussed under the head of "Canon Law," in Stephens' *Laws Relating to the Clergy*, Vol. I., pp. 223-7. *Cf.* also Phillimore's *Ecclesiastical Law*, Vol. II., p. 1562 ; Blunt's *Church Law*, p. 23.

SUMMARY OF THE PRINCIPAL JUDGMENTS RELATING TO THE ORNAMENTS OF THE MINISTER AND THE CHURCH, 1845-1906

SUMMARY OF THE PRINCIPAL JUDGMENTS RELATING TO THE ORNAMENTS OF THE MINISTER AND THE CHURCH, 1845—1906.

Date.	Name of Suit and Church.	Reference.	Court and Judge.	Points Decided.	
				Illegal.	Legal.
1845.	*Faulkner v. Litchfield.* [Holy Sepulchre, Cambridge.]	1 Robertson's Ecclesiastical Reports, p. 184.	Court of Arches. Sir Herbert Jenner-Fust, on Appeal from Chancellor of Ely.	1. Stone altar. 2. Credence table.	
1855. Dec. 5.	*Westerton v. Liddell. Beal v. Liddell.* [St. Paul's, Knightsbridge, and St. Barnabas', Pimlico.] [Consolidated suits.]	1 Jur., N. S. 1178. Moore's Special Report.	Consistory Court of London. Dr. Lushington.	1. Stone altar. 2. Credence table [following *Faulkner v. Litchfield*]. 3. Cross on altar and cross on rood screen. 4. Lighted candles on communion table, when not required for purpose of light. 5. Coloured altar cloths. *Note.*—Chancel gates and screen were held to be "objectionable," but were not ordered to be removed. The Ten Commandments were ordered by the Court to be set up at the East end of the chancel, there being "no discretionary power to substitute the end of the nave for the end of the chancel." It was assumed by Dr. Lushington that *crucifixes* were prohibited, and the Privy Council in sanctioning *crosses* carefully drew a distinction between the two. Crucifixes were disallowed by Lord Penzance in *Clifton v. Ridsdale*, 1 P. D 316, and on appeal by the Privy Council ; by Dr. Tristram, Chancellor of London, in the cases of *In re St. Mark's, Marylebone,* [1897] P. 114, *Kensit and others v. the Rector and Churchwardens of St. Ethelburga, Bishopsgate Within,* [1900] P. 80, *Davey v. Hinde,* [1901] P. 95 ; by Chancellor	1. Lighted candles on communion table, when so required.
,,	,,	p. 77.			
,,	,,	p. 54.			

Date	Case	Reference	Court	Judgment / Remarks
1856. Dec. 20.	" "	p. 85.	Court of Arches. (On Appeal.) Sir John Dodson.	Kempe in *Markham v. Vicar, &c., of Shirebrook*, [1906] P. 389; by Chancellor Espin in *Brockman and others v. All of St. John the Baptist, West Derby*, 1902; and in *In re St. Mary's, Chester*, 1906. Judgment affirmed on all points.
1857. Mar. 21.	*Liddell v. Westerton.* *Liddell v. Beal.*	Moore's Special Report, p. 149.	Judicial Committee of the Privy Council. Lord Cranworth (Lord Chancellor) Lord Wensleydale Pemberton Leigh Sir John Patteson Sir Wm. Maule Abp. Cantuar (Sumner) Bp. of London (Tait)	*Judgment delivered by Pemberton Leigh.* 1. Stone altars. 2. Cross attached to communion table. 3. Embroidery and lace on "fair white linen cloth." *Remarks:* It was in this judgment, in discussing variations in the form of the Ornaments Rubric in Elizabeth's and subsequent Prayer Books, that the famous *obiter dictum* was uttered: "They all obviously mean the same thing, that the *same dresses and the same utensils, or articles, which were used under the First Prayer Book of Edward the Sixth may still be used.*" In discussing the meaning of "By authority of Parliament, in the second year of the reign of King Edward the Sixth," the Privy Council held that this must refer to the First Prayer Book, . . . "its use, and the injunctions contained in it, were established by authority of Parliament in the second year of Edward the Sixth, and *this is the plain meaning of the Rubric.*" *Vide* Moore's Special Report, pp. 159, 160. On the whole the High Church party won in the first suit before the Privy Council. The case went to the ornaments of the *Church* only. 1. Crosses as *architectural decorations.* Cross on chancel screen. 2. Credence table (small side table on which elements are placed before consecration). 3. Embroidered and coloured altar cloths.
1868. Mar. 28.	*Martin v. Mackonochie.* *Flamank v. Simpson.* [St. Alban's, Holborn, and East Teignmouth.] [Consolidated suits.]	L. R. 2 Adm. and Eccl. p. 116. p. 215.	Court of Arches. Sir Robert Phillimore. [By letters of request from Bishops of London and Exeter.]	1. Elevation of paten and cup above the head after consecration of the elements. 2. To bring in *incense* at the beginning or during, and to	"Excessive kneeling" a matter for the Bishop's discretion. [The *ceremonial* or *liturgical* use of incense was condemned

DATE.	NAME OF SUIT AND CHURCH.	REFERENCE.	COURT AND JUDGE.	POINTS DECIDED. ILLEGAL.	POINTS DECIDED. LEGAL.
1868.	*Martin v. Mackonochie.* *Flamank v. Simpson.*	L. R 2 Adm. and Eccl. p. 116. p. 215.	Court of Arches.	remove it at the close of the celebration, is unlawful as "*a distinct ceremony*," additional and not even indirectly incident to the ceremonies ordered by the Book of Common Prayer," though it be "*an ancient, innocent, and pleasing custom.*" 3. To mix water with the wine during celebration. 4. To place alms upon a stool instead of upon Holy Table. [In the case of Mr. Simpson only. An insignificant point, at once conceded.]	as contrary to 1 Eliz. c. 2, by the Archbishops of Canterbury (Temple) and York (Maclagan) at their "Hearing," July 31, 1899.] But *Quære*: Whether it is illegal to administer wine with which a little water has been *previously mixed.* 1. *Two lights* upon the Holy Table during the time of Holy Communion "for the signification that Christ is the very true light of the world." Lawful under the *Injunctions* of 1547, which Sir R. Phillimore held to be *unrepealed.*
		p. 244.		*Remarks*: In the Arches Court the gains and losses of the two parties were about equal.	
1868. Dec. 23.	*Martin v. Mackonochie.* [No appeal was lodged in the case of *Flamank v. Simpson.*]	L. R. 2 Privy Council Cases, p. 365. p. 385.	Judicial Committee of Privy Council. Appeal by promoter on points decided to be lawful by Arches Court. Lord Cairns (Lord Chancellor). Abp. York (Thomson).	*Judgment delivered by Lord Cairns.* The Judgment of the Court of Arches reversed on all points on which it was favourable to the Respondent. 1. *Kneeling or prostrating* himself before the Consecrated Elements during prayer of Consecration. Does not come within the discretion of Bishop to allow	[Overruling Sir R. Phillimore.]

Lord Chelmsford. Lord Westbury. Sir Wm. Erle (Chief Justice of the Common Pleas). Sir Jas. Colville.	or disallow under Preface to Prayer-book. 2. *Lighted candles* on Holy Table during the celebration of Holy Communion unlawful. (1) As being an additional ceremony prohibited by Elizabeth's Act of Uniformity, 1 Eliz. c. 2, ss. 4 and 27, which *repealed the Injunctions* of Edward VI. (2) Because not Ornaments within the meaning of Ornaments Rubric. The Privy Council drew a distinction between the "inert" use of ornaments, which might be innocent as part of the "furniture of the church, and the "active" use of the same things, which converted them into ceremonies. Thus the "lighting, cremation, and symbolical use" of candles could only be "justified, if at all, as part of the ceremonial law." *Remarks:* The principle that "*Omission is prohibition*" was first laid down in this case. V. remarks of Sir R. Phillimore at p. 218 of 2 A. and E., on the mixed chalice, "in my opinion the legal consequence of this *omission*, both of the water and of the act of mixing it with the wine, must be considered as a *prohibition* of the ceremony." "My decision upon this point is that the mixing would be a ceremony *designedly omitted in and therefore prohibited* by the rubrics of the present Prayer Book." V. also Judgment of Privy Council, at p. 391 of 2 Privy Council Cases. "They [lighted candles] are not subsidiary to the service, ... nor can a separate and independent Ornament, previously in use, be said to be consistent with a Rubric which is silent as to it, and which *by necessary implication abolishes what it does not retain.*" In the result, the Low Church Party won all along the line. *The Respondent was represented by Counsel in both Courts.*	[Overruling Sir R. Phillimore on this point.]

DATE.	NAME OF SUIT AND CHURCH.	REFERENCE.	COURT AND JUDGE.	POINTS DECIDED.	
				ILLEGAL.	LEGAL.
1870. Feb. 3.	*Sumner v. Wix.* [St. Michael and All Angels, Swanmore, Diocese of Winchester.]	L. R. 3 A. & E. 58.	Court of Arches. Sir R. Phillimore. [By letters of request from Bp. of Winchester.]	1. Lighted candles held on each side of priest during reading of Gospel. 2. The *ceremonial lighting and burning of candles* placed on a shelf or ledge over the Holy Table, and of candles placed on the ground on each side of the Holy Table during the Communion service. 3. The *ceremonial use of incense* immediately before and so as to be preparatory or subsidiary to the celebration of Holy Communion.	[Substantially the same point as that on "processional lights," raised at the Archbishops, "Hearing" in June, 1899, and held to be illegal by the Archbishops as contrary to the Elizabethan Act of Uniformity, 1 Eliz. c. 2., July 31, 1899.] [The *fumigatory* use of incense "to sweeten the church," provided the use be "outside public worship," was allowed by the Archbishops of Canterbury and York at their "Hearing," July 31, 1899.]
1870. Feb. 3.	*Elphinstone v. Purchas.* [St. James's Chapel, in Parish of Brighton.]	L. R. 3 A. & E. 66.	Court of Arches. Sir R. Phillimore. [By letters of request from Bishop of Chichester.]	*No appeal lodged. Defendant appeared by Counsel.* 1. The cope, except at the Communion service. 2. Albs with patches called *apparels*, tippets of a circular form, stoles, dalmatics, and maniples. 3. *Processions* so conducted as to constitute a rite or ceremony. 4. The *crucifix* and banners held during service as a matter of ceremony.	1. The *Eucharistic vestments* enjoined by the First Prayer-book of Edward VI., *i.e.,* the cope, chasuble, white alb plain, surplice, tunicle. 2. The *biretta* as a protection to the head when needed. 3. Administration of water and wine *previously mingled.* 4. *Wafer bread*, circular in form provided it be *broken*, as the rubric directs.

5. Distribution of *ashes* on Ash Wednesday.
6. Censing and sprinkling with holy water, candles lighted and distributed to congregation on Candlemas Day.
7. Ringing of *Sacring bell* during Consecration prayer.
8. Singing of *Agnus Dei* after Prayer of Consecration.
9. Giving notice of and celebrating a "*mortuary celebration*."
10. Ceremonial admission of acolyte before Evening Service.
11. Censing crucifix above Holy Table.
12. *Lighted candles* on Holy Table during the celebration of Holy Communion as matter of ceremony.
13. Use of *incense* for censing persons and things.
14. Ceremonial mixing of wine with water.
15. Elevation of paten and cup.
16. Elevation of alms dish and removal to credence table.
17. Use of *Paschal candle*. Bearing about, moving, setting down, and lifting up as matters of ceremony lighted candles when not required for purpose of light.
18. *Crucifix placed on ledge* in

5. Decoration of Holy Table with vases of flowers. Held to be an "innocent and not unseemly decoration." On a par with holly at Christmas.
6. Eastward position during Prayer of Consecration.

[Sir R. Phillimore had pronounced this legal in *Martin v. Mackonochie*, but was overruled by Privy Council.]
[Incense already condemned in *Martin v. Mackonochie* and *Sumner v. Wix*.]

[Condemned in *Martin v. Mackonochie*.]

[Substantially the same charge as in *Sumner v. Wix*.]

Date.	Name of Suit and Church.	Reference.	Court and Judge.	Points decided.	
				Illegal.	Legal.
1870. Feb 3.	*Elphinstone v. Purchas.*	L. R. 3 A & E. 66.	Court of Arches.	connexion with Holy Table not being part of the architectural decoration of the church. *Covering* same during Lent and on Good Friday, and *uncovering* on Easter Day. 19. Bowing to crucifix. 20. Placing of modelled figure of infant Saviour with two lilies in the Church at Christmas. Placing figure, image, or stuffed skin of a dove over Holy Table at Whitsuntide. 21. Permitting Holy Table to remain without any decent covering, as required by Canon 82, on Good Friday. 22. Making Sign of the Cross. 23. Kissing the Book of the Gospels. 24. Eastward Position during Prayer for Church Militant. Elevating chalice at the word "oblations." 25. Eastward Position during reading of Collects before the epistle for the day. 26. Giving notice of Saints' days and holy days for which no service is provided by Prayer-book.	

1871. Feb. 23.	Hebbert v. Purchas. [The original Appellant Elphinstone having died, the Appellant Hebbert was by leave of the Privy Council substituted as Promoter in his place. L. R. 3 P. C. 245.]	L. R. 3 Privy Council Cases, 605.

Judicial Committee.
Lord Hatherley (Lord Chancellor)
Abp. of York (Thomson)
Bp. of London (Jackson)
Lord Chelmsford
Judgment delivered by Lord Hatherley.

1. Chasuble, Alb, and Tunicle.
2. Eastward Position at Prayer of Consecration.
3. Wafer Bread.
4. Administration of Mixed Chalice.
5. *Quære.* Biretta.

1. Use of *Cope* in Cathedral and Collegiate Churches at Holy Communion by the "principal minister."

Remarks:
The *Defendant alleging poverty did not appear* by Counsel and the case was undefended. Many of the points alleged were of minor importance. The important points are that Sir R. Phillimore *sanctioned the use of the Edwardian vestments*, Eastward position during Prayer of Consecration, wafer bread, and administration of mixed chalice, and forbade ceremonial processions. He was of opinion that the Elizabethan *Advertisements* of 1566 never had legal validity, and therefore did not modify the Ornaments Rubric. This was the first case in which the Ornaments of the *Minister* came into question. Dealing with the argument from the admitted disuse of the vestments as affording a *contemporanea expositio* of the Ornaments Rubric, the learned judge said at p. 91 :—" In truth the argument is bad, as proving a great deal too much. The same argument would make the copes in the cathedrals unlawful, which it is admitted they are not; the use of the surplice in preaching unlawful, which is the proper dress; and, *e converso*, would establish the legality of the use of the *black gown, which has no warrant of law.* . . ."
The latter dictum was disapproved of by the Court of Appeal (in *In re Robinson, Wright v. Tugwell*, [1897] 1 Ch. 85). V. p. 133.

Remarks:
The judgment of Sir R. Phillimore was reversed on all points on which it had been favourable to the Respondent.
The Privy Council decided against Vestments on the ground that the Ornaments Rubric had to that extent been superseded by the *Advertisements of Elizabeth* (1566) dealing with the Vestures of the Clergy, the Canons of 1603, and the Act of Uniformity of Charles II. The whole matter was elaborately

Date.	Name of Suit and Church.	Reference.	Court and Judge.	Points decided. Illegal.	Points decided. Legal.
1871. Feb. 23.	*Hebbert v. Purchas.*	L. R. 3 Privy Council Cases, 605.	Judicial Committee.		discussed by Lord Hatherley in this case and Lord Cairns in *Ridsdale v. Clifton*, whose judgments were afterwards subjected to damaging criticism in a series of pamphlets by Mr. James Parker, of Oxford. Lord Selborne wrote a learned pamphlet in defence of the view put forward by the Judicial Committee. Though the law was authoritatively declared by the Privy Council, the controversy has never been closed, and the Judicial Committee itself might be led to a different view if the matter were ever re-argued before it. V. *Separate note on the Advertisements*, p. 132.
1873. Dec. 15.	*White v. Bowron.* [St. Barnabas, Pimlico.]	L. R. 4 A. & E. 207. Tristram's Consistory Judgments, 1.	Consistory Court of London. Dr. Tristram.		*Baldacchino* or canopy of marble over the Holy Table, because not an ornament within the meaning of the "Ornaments Rubric," nor consistent with and subsidiary to the service. Not a mere architectural adornment.
1874. Dec. 7.	*Martin v. Mackonochie.* [Second suit.] [St. Alban's, Holborn.]	L. R. 4 A. & E. 279.	Court of Arches. Sir R. Phillimore. [By letters of request from the Bp. of London.]	Defendant was admonished and suspended for six weeks for having contravened the judgment of the Arches Court and the Privy Council in the following points: 1. Lighted candles on Communion Table. 2. Do. carried about. 3. Processions with banners and illegal vestments. 4. Wearing alb, cope, chasuble, amice or maniple, stole, and girdle. 5. Eastward position during Prayer of Consecration.	

Date	Case	Reference	Court	Subject and Remarks
1874. Aug. 6.	Boyd v. Philpotts. (Exeter Cathedral.)	L. R. 4 A. & E. 297.	Court of Arches. Sir Robert Phillimore.	5. Wafer bread. 6. Agnus Dei. 7. Sign of Cross made towards the congregation. 8. Kissing the Service-book. *Remarks:* The Defendant, who *appeared by Counsel*, did not appeal. Sir R. Phillimore considered 'that the judgment of the Privy Council in *Hebbert v. Purchas* was irreconcilable with its previous decisions in *Westerton v. Liddell* and *Martin v. Mackonochie* (first suit), but thought that any new argument would be more properly addressed to the Privy Council itself. N.B.—All these cases were brought under the old *Church Discipline Act* of 1840, 3 and 4 Vict. c. 86. A reredos with sculptural re-presentations in bas-relief of the Ascension, Transfiguration, and Descent of the Holy Ghost at Pentecost. *Remarks:* Sir R. Phillimore reversed the decision of the Bishop of Exeter (Temple), who as Visitor of the Cathedral, sitting with Mr. Justice Keating as assessor, had condemned the structure as illegal, and had ordered a plain metal screen with the Ten Commandments to be set up in its stead, and decided that the Bishop had no power to order the removal.
1875. Feb. 25.	Philpotts v. Boyd.	L.R. 6 Privy Council Cases 435.	Judicial Committee. Lord Hatherley. Lord Penzance Lord Selborne Sir Fitzroy Kelly (Lord Chief Baron) Sir Montague Smith Sir Robert Collier.	Judgment delivered by Lord Hatherley. *Reredos lawful as decoration,* and as not being liable to superstitious abuse. Sir R. Phillimore's judgment reversed so far as related to Bishop's jurisdiction. [*Note.*—What is known as "the St. Paul's reredos case," *Reg. v. Bishop of London,* 23 Q. B. D. 414; 24 Q. B. D. 213, (1889), went only to the meaning of the words "after considering the whole circumstances of the case" in s. 9 of 37 and 38 Vict. c. 85.]

Date.	Name of Suit and Church.	Reference.	Court and Judge.	Points decided. Illegal. / Legal.
1874. Nov. 27.	*Combe v. Edwards.* [Prestbury—Diocese of Gloucester and Bristol.]	L.R. 4 A. & E. 390.	Court of Arches. Sir R. Phillimore.	*Remarks:* The case (which was brought under the Church Discipline Act, 1840) established no new point as to ritual. The articles charged: 1. Lighted candles. 2. Eastward position. 3. Elevation of paten, &c. 4. Wafer bread. 5. Mixed chalice. 6. Genuflection and prostration during Prayer of Consecration. 7. Sign of the Cross in administration of elements. 8. Crucifix on ledge above Holy Table (struck out by order of the Court). 9. Eucharistic vestments. In May, 1876, the case came before Lord Penzance, who on July 17, 1877, held that he was bound to follow the decision of the Privy Council in *Ridsdale v. Clifton* as to vestments (given since the commencement of this suit), and admonished the defendant on all the points complained of.
1876. Feb. 26.	*Clifton v. Ridsdale.* [St. Peter's, Folkestone, Diocese of Canterbury.]	1 Probate Division, 316.	Court of Arches. [Held to be so in *Ex parte Dale* and *Ex parte Enraght*, 6 Q. B. D. 376.] Lord Penzance.	*Note.—The Public Worship Regulation Act*, 37 and 38 Vict., c. 85, was passed August 7, 1874. It came into operation on July 1, 1875. Lord Penzance was appointed Judge under the Statute, Oct. 28, 1874, and succeeded by force of the Statute to the office of Dean of the Arches on the resignation of Sir R. Phillimore, Oct. 20, 1875, and to the Judgeship of the Chancery Court of York on the resignation of Mr. Granville Harcourt Vernon, Oct. 30, 1875. He refused to take the oaths and subscribe the Thirty-Nine Articles as required by Canon 127, and his Court, though declared by the Queen's Bench and House of Lords to be, and to have the authority of, the old Court of Arches, was never acknowledged as such by the High Church Party. The scrupulous care taken to secure the canonical status of subsequent Deans of the Arches, Sir Arthur Charles and Sir Lewis Dibdin, goes far to prove that the High Church clergy were right in their contention on this point. The charges were: 1. Lighted candles. 2. Alb and chasuble.

Date	Case	Citation	Judges	Practices charged	Decision
1877. May 12.	Ridsdale v. Clifton.	2 P. D. 276.	Judicial Committee. Lord Cairns (Lord Chancellor) Lord Selborne Sir Jas. Colvile Lord Chief Baron Kelly. Sir R. Phillimore Lord Justice James Sir Montague Smith Sir Robert Collier	3. Mixed chalice. 4. Wafer bread. 5. Eastward position during Prayer of Consecration, so as to prevent people seeing manual acts. 6. Twice unlawfully kneeling during Prayer of Consecration. 7. Agnus Dei. 8. Celebrating with only one communicant. 9. Processions. 10. Crucifix and 24 metal candlesticks on rood screen. 11. Stations of the Cross. Defendant *admonished* to refrain from practices 1—9. *Crucifix ordered to be* removed, as being liable to "superstitious reverence," and not a mere architectural decoration. *Stations of the Cross* declared illegal, and ordered to be removed. Appeal by Ridsdale on: (1) Vestments. (2) Eastward position. (3) Wafer bread. (4) Crucifix. Judgment of Court below affirmed on points (1) and (4), but as to (2) "so standing that in good faith the bulk of the communicants	(1) Eastward position during Prayer of Consecration, *provided that the manual acts are visible.*

Date.	Name of Suit and Church.	Reference.	Court and Judge.	Points Decided. Illegal.	Points Decided. Legal.
1877. May 12.	Ridsdale v. Clifton.	2 P. D. 276.	Judicial Committee. Sir Baliol Brett Sir R. Amphlett Assessors.—Abp. Cantuar (Tait), Bps. of Chichester (Durnford), St. Asaph (Hughes), Ely (Woodford), St. David's Jones).		can see the manual acts" is made the criterion of legality: and as to (3) the *composition, not the shape*, of the wafer is the test.

Remarks:
Ridsdale appeared before Lord Penzance by Counsel, and *himself appealed* to the Privy Council, the first and only instance, after the passing of the Public Worship Regulation Act, in which a clergyman accused of Ritual offences acknowledged the jurisdiction of either Court. The suits in which five clergymen—Dale, Tooth, Enraght, Green, and Bell-Cox—were committed to prison for contempt, were all *undefended*. The offences charged were similar to those in the earlier cases, and the later suits have *no importance as to the law of Ritual*, but only as to certain points relating to procedure, the status, and jurisdiction of Lord Penzance's Court, &c. Procedure under the Public Worship Regulation Act having been found to be cumbrous and slow in operation, the last of these suits, *Hakes v. Cox*, [1892] P. 110, was in 1885 brought under the old *Church Discipline Act* of 1840, 3 and 4 Vict., c. 86. The suit became a leading case on the law of *Habeas Corpus*.

The *Ridsdale case*, in conjunction with the *Mackonochie and Purchas judgments*, defined the law of the Church as interpreted by the Privy Council. The effect of the *Elizabethan Advertisements* was again examined and discussed in a very learned judgment delivered by Lord Cairns.

Three members of the Committee, Sir R. Phillimore, Sir R. Amphlett and Lord Chief Baron Kelly, *are known to have dissented*, but Lord Cairns as Chancellor issued an order, founded on an older order of the Privy Council, in Charles I.'s reign,

1876.
July 11.	*Durst v. Masters.*
[St. Margaret, King's Lynn. Diocese of Norwich.]	1 P. D. 123, 373.	*Judicial Committee* on appeal from Court of Arches.
Lord Cairns
Lord Hatherley
Lord Penzance
Sir Barnes Peacock
Sir Montague Smith.	forbidding the public expression of such dissent. Sir Fitzroy Kelly published a pamphlet to prove that Lord Cairns's action was *illegal and unconstitutional*, which was cogently argued in a book issued soon after by *W. F. Finlason*, a Roman Catholic, and a very learned authority on constitutional law. Lord Cairns's argument on the effect of the Advertisements is a masterpiece of close and careful reasoning, in which the grounds on which the validity of the Advertisements is asserted or denied, are weighed and passed in review. But his reasoning was never accepted by the High Church party, who were further exasperated by what they held to be the "gagging" of the minority, who desired that the fact of their dissent should be openly and publicly made known. Permission to issue *separate judgments*, after the manner of the King's Bench and House of Lords, would tend to allay discontent and strengthen the public confidence in the findings of the Committee. In any future readjustment of the final Court of Appeal in ecclesiastical cases on the lines of the existing Court, it is now generally recognised that this right must be conceded. *Vide* recommendation of the Ecclesiastical Courts Commission, 1883, p. 58.
Sir Fitzroy Kelly stigmatised the judgment in the famous phrase "*a judgment of policy not of law*," and was severely criticised by Lord Selborne for so doing. V. Selborne's Memoirs, 2nd Series. Vol. I., Chap. XVII
The law as at present defined rests upon this inconclusive judgment.	Moveable wooden *cross* placed on *retable* or wooden ledge at the back of and immediately above the Communion Table.

127

Date.	Name of Suit and Church.	Reference.	Court and Judge.	Points Decided. Illegal.	Points Decided. Legal.
1877. May 14.	*In re St. Augustine, Haggerstone.* [Heard and decided together]	4 P. D. 111. Tristram's Consistory Judgments, 60.	Consistory Court of London. Dr. Tristram.	Chancel *Gates*.	Dwarf wall between Chancel and Nave.
1877. May 14.	*Vicar of Parish of the Annunciation, Chislehurst, v. Parishioners of same.*	4 P. D. 114, Tristram's Consistory Judgments, 67.	Commissary Court of Canterbury. Dr. Tristram.	Chancel *Gates*.	Chancel *Screen* without cross.
1877. June 18.	*Hughes v. Edwards.* [St. Mary's, Denbigh.]	2 P. D. 361.	Court of Arches. Lord Penzance. By letters of request from Official Principal of Bishop of St. Asaph.		Reredos containing representation of *Crucifixion* with figure of our *Saviour on the Cross*, *St. John*, and the *Three Marys*.
1878. Nov. 28.	*Bradford v. Fry.* [St. James's, Hatcham.]	4 P. D. 93.	Court of Arches, Lord Penzance, on Appeal from Chancellor of Rochester.	Chancel *Gates*.	Chancel *Screen* without gates.
1880. Feb. 16.	*Woodward, Clerk, and Others v. Parishioners of Folkestone.*	Tristram's Consistory Judgments, 177.	Commissary Court of Canterbury. Dr. Tristram.	Faculty refused for design for *painted window* representing a *priest habited in Eucharistic vestments* prohibited to be worn by the English clergy.	
1880. Mar. 18.	*In re St. Lawrence, Pittington.*	5 P. D. 131.	Consistory Court of Durham. H. Cowie.	Faculty refused for paintings on reredos representing *Our Lord in Glory*, the *Blessed Virgin*, *St. John*, *St. Stephen*, *and St. Lawrence*, on the ground that	

Date	Case	Reference	Court		Result
				there was danger of "adoration" or "superstitious reverence" being paid to them.	
1885. Nov. 3.	*In re St. Agnes, Toxteth Park.*	11 P. D. 1.	Consistory Court of Liverpool. Rev. T. E. Espin, D.D., D.C.L.		Faculty granted for Chancel *Gates*, on the ground that the "great richness and excellence of the ornaments of the chancel" rendered some protection necessary.
1887. June 19.	*In re Holy Trinity Church, Stroud Green.*	12 P. D. 199. 36 W. R. 288.	Consistory Court of London. Dr. Tristram.		*Second Holy Table* in side chapel for "greater convenience and diminution of expense." A lawful Ornament because subsidiary to the performance of Divine service.
1888. July 5.	*In re Church of St. John, Isle of Dogs.*	4 Times Law Reports, 661. Tristram's Consistory Judgments, 67	Consistory Court of London. Dr. Tristram.		Faculty granted for Chancel Screen *with Gates*, on the ground that they were necessary for the protection of music books and other property.
1889. June 3.	*In re St. George's, Jesmond.*	*Law Journal*, June 22, 1889, pp. 375–8; *Guardian*, June 5, 1889, pp. 881–2.	Consistory Court of Newcastle. A. B. Kempe, M.A.	Faculty for *second Holy Table* refused on general ground of illegality. Not a matter of discretion.	
1889. Aug. 16.	*In re St Paul's, Wilton Place.*	Tristram's Consistory Judgments, 120.	Consistory Court of London. Dr. Tristram.		Faculty granted for construction of side chapel with *second Holy Table*, conditional on the chapel being separated from the church by a screen.

DATE.	NAME OF SUIT AND CHURCH.	REFERENCE.	COURT AND JUDGE.	POINTS DECIDED. ILLEGAL.	POINTS DECIDED. LEGAL.
1890. April 5.	*In re Holy Trinity*, Hastings.	*Law Journal*, May 10, May 17, 1890, pp. 284-6, and 298-300.	Consistory Court of Chichester. R. W. Wintle.	Faculty refused for *second Holy Table* either in an aisle or side chapel.	
1890. Nov. 21.	*Read v. Bp. of Lincoln.* [St. Peter at Gowts, Lincoln.] [The Privy Council held that the Archbishop had jurisdiction to cite a bishop in *Ex parte Read*, 13 P. D. 221, Aug. 3, 1888].	Roscoe's Report, 1891, p. 9. 14 P. D. 88, 148. [1891] P. 9.	Court of the Archbishop of Canterbury. Abp. Cantuar (Benson). *Assessors.*—Bps. of London (Temple), Hereford (Atlay), Rochester (Thorold), Oxford (Stubbs), Salisbury (Wordsworth), and the Vicar-General (Sir J. Parker Deane).	1. Mixing water with wine in and as part of the service. 2. So to stand that Communicants cannot see manual acts. 3. Sign of the Cross while pronouncing the Absolution and Benediction (because an additional ceremony).	1. Two lighted candles not required for purposes of light standing on the Holy Table continuously during service. 2. Administering chalice previously mixed. 3. Eastward position prior to Prayer of Consecration. 4. Agnus Dei. 5. Ablutions (pouring wine and water into cup and drinking the "rinsings" at end of service.) [No part of the service and not an additional ceremony].
1892. Aug. 2.	*Read v. Bp. of Lincoln.*	[1892] Appeal Cases, 644.	Judicial Committee. Lord Halsbury (Lord Chancellor) Lord Hobhouse Lord Esher (M. R.) Lord Herschell Lord Hannen Sir Richard Couch Lord Shand *Assessors.*—Bishop of Chichester (Durnford),	*Remarks:* The Appeal was dismissed and the judgment of the Archbishop	1. Administering chalice previously mixed. 2. Agnus Dei. 3. Eastward position from commencement of Communion service to the ordering of bread and wine before Prayer of Consecration.

St. David's (Jones), Lichfield (Maclagan). *Judgment delivered by Lord Halsbury.*

affirmed on all points, except that with regard to altar lights the Committee expressed no opinion, holding that, officiating in a strange church, the Bishop was not responsible for their being alight. The earlier judgment of the Privy Council in *Martin v. Mackonochie* condemning lighted candles therefore still stands. The Bishop appeared under protest to the jurisdiction before the Archbishop of Canterbury, but refused to be represented by Counsel before the Privy Council.

By his protest he asserted that the primitive, constitutional, and canonical Court to try him was *not the Metropolitan sitting alone*, or with Assessors only, but the *Metropolitan with all the comprovincial Bishops, i.e.,* the Upper House of the Synod of the Province. This, after argument, was ruled by the Archbishop against him, and the Bishop then submitted to the judgment of the Court.

The administration of the *mixed chalice* had been condemned by the Privy Council in *Hebbert v. Purchas.*

The *Agnus Dei* was pronounced illegal by the Court of Arches in *Elphinstone v. Purchas.* On this point there had been no previous decision of the Privy Council.

The *Eastward position during the Prayer of Consecration* had been held to be illegal by the Privy Council in *Hebbert v. Purchas* but sanctioned in *Ridsdale v. Clifton,* provided the manual acts were visible.

In the Lincoln case they say, at p. 665, "Their Lordships consider that it (the Rubric) cannot be regarded as so definitely and unequivocally enjoining that the priest shall, no matter how the table may be placed, stand at that end of the table which faces the north when saying the opening prayers, that no other position can be assumed without the commission of an ecclesiastical offence.... All that they determine is that it is *not an ecclesiastical offence to stand at the northern part of the side which faces westwards.*"

On the *mixed chalice* they found themselves "unable to concur in Lord Hatherley's reasoning" in *Hebbert v. Purchas.*

The right and duty of the Committee to re-open any question decided by their predecessors, if "fresh light" could be brought to bear upon it, was affirmed in *Ridsdale v. Clifton* and *Read v. Bishop of Lincoln.*

NOTE ON THE ORNAMENTS RUBRIC AND THE ADVERTISEMENTS OF ELIZABETH.

The Privy Council in *Westerton v. Liddell* decided that the "authority of Parliament" referred to in the Rubric was the first Act of Uniformity of Edward VI. (2 and 3 Ed. VI., c. 1), which established the First Prayer-book, and not the Act of Henry VIII. (25 Henry VIII., c. 19), which kept alive the old Canon Law, and certain Injunctions of Henry and Edward. [This point was re-argued before the Archbishops at their "Hearing," May, 1899.]

The First Prayer-book of Edward VI. ordered the use of the "white albe plain, with a vestment (*i.e.*, a chasuble) or cope" for the principal minister at the Communion, and "albes with tunicles" for the two assistants.

S. 25 of 1 Eliz., c. 2 (Act of Uniformity), said that such Ornaments of the Church and Minister were to be retained and be in use "as was in this Church of England, by authority of Parliament, in the second year of the reign of King Edward VI., until *other order* shall be taken by the authority of the Queen's Majesty, with the advice of the Commissioners appointed and authorised under the Great Seal of England, or of the Metropolitan of this realm."

This section was embodied in a Note or Rubric prefixed to the Prayer-book of Elizabeth, and re-enacted with slight verbal modifications at the Revision of 1662, our present "Ornaments Rubric."

In 1565 Elizabeth wrote a letter to Archbishop Parker requiring him to issue certain orders to the clergy upon vestures among other things. Parker drew up the Advertisements in consequence, but the Queen, frightened by the Puritan party, or from some other cause, *is believed never to have ratified them*. Nevertheless, they were issued by the Bishops, referred to as authoritative in Visitation Articles, the Canons of 1571 and 1603, and everywhere acted upon. The Privy Council in *Ridsdale v. Clifton* held that the Queen's authority must be presumed to have been given.

The words of the Advertisements in question are as follows:

"Item, In ministration of the holy communion in the Cathedral and collegiate churches, the principal minister shall use a cope with gospeller and epistoler agreeably; and at all other prayers to be sayde at the communion table, to use no copes but surplesses."

"Item, That every minister sayinge any public prayers, or ministringe the Sacraments, or other rites of the Churche, shall wear a comely surples with sleeves, to be provided at the charges of the parish. . . ."

The whole controversy, so far as the Ornaments of the *Minister* are concerned, turns upon (1) whether the Advertisements *ever had legal validity* under the statute authorising the "taking of other order"; and (2) whether, granted that they amounted to such "taking of other order," the obligation to use the surplice superseded the use of the Edwardian Vestments.

Lord Hatherley in *Hebbert v. Purchas*, and Lord Cairns in *Ridsdale v. Clifton*, answered in the affirmative, and disallowed the vestments, admittedly required by the Rubric, on that ground.

Historical investigation goes to show that, in dealing with Puritan defaulters, the surplice was enjoined by the Advertisements as the *minimum* vesture of the clergy.

DATE.	NAME OF SUIT AND CHURCH.	REFERENCE.	COURT AND JUDGE.	POINTS DECIDED.	
				ILLEGAL.	LEGAL.
1891. Nov. 3.	*In re Robinson, Wright v. Tugwell.* [St. John the Evangelist, Boscombe.]	[1892] 1 Ch. 95	Chancery Division, High Court of Justice. North, J.		Black gown in the pulpit when preaching, the legality of the black gown in preaching being sanctioned by the continuous usage of centuries, uncontrolled by positive law or judicial decision.
1896. Nov. 28.	*In re Robinson, Wright v. Tugwell.*	[1897] 1 Ch. 85	Court of Appeal. Lord Russell of Killowen, C.J. Lindley and A. L. Smith, L.JJ.		Dictum of Sir R. Phillimore in *Elphinstone v. Purchas*, L. R. 3 A. and E. at p. 91, disapproved of. V. p. 121.
1894. April 6.	Rector and Churchwardens of St. Andrew's, Romford, *v.* All having interest.	[1894] Probate, 220.	Consistory Court of St. Albans. A. B. Kempe, M.A.	Chancel *Gates* refused under *Bradford v. Fry.*	
1894. April 26.	Vicar and Churchwardens of St. James, Norland *v.* Parishioners of the same.	[1894] P. 256.	Consistory Court of London. Dr. Tristram.		Gates to a Chancel screen sanctioned on the ground of *utility.*
1894. Aug. 22	Vicar and Churchwardens of St. Peter's, Eaton Square, *v.* Parishioners of same.	[1894] P. 350.	Consistory Court of London. Dr. Tristram.		Chancel screen *with gates.* *Second Holy Table,* provided the side chapel be separated from the main chancel by a screen of open trellis work.
1894. Nov. 10.	Vicar and Churchwardens of St. John the Baptist, Timberhill *v.* The Rectors, Impropriators, Parishioners, etc., of same.	[1895] P. 71.	Consistory Court of Norwich. T. C. Blofeld, M.A.	Confirmatory faculty refused for figures of *Our Lord* with SS. *Mary and John* on beam above Chancel screen. Faculty refused for additional figures of *St. Mary Magda-*	Faculty granted for Chancel screen, *with gates,* and for screens across the aisles, also with gates.

Date.	Name of Suit and Church.	Reference.	Court and Judge.	Points Decided.	
				Illegal.	Legal.
1894. Nov. 10.	Vicar and Churchwardens of St. John the Baptist, Timberhill, v. The Rectors, Impropriators, Parishioners, etc., of same.	[1895] P. 71.	Consistory Court of Norwich. T. C. Blofeld, M.A.	lene and the Centurion, on the ground that there was danger of "superstitious reverence" being paid to the rood, there being evidence to show that unauthorised services had been held in connexion with the figures.	
1895. Feb. 1.	Vicar and Churchwardens of St. John, Pendlebury v. Parishioners of same.	[1895] P. 178.	Consistory Court of Manchester. P. V. Smith, LL.D.		Faculty granted for triptych with painted panels representing Last Supper, Agony in the Garden, and Risen Christ with Marys at the tomb, surmounted by carved oak figures of Our Lord, Moses, and Elias, provided that the triptych was always to remain open during the time of divine service.
1896. May 29.	Rector and Churchwarden of Barsham v. Parishioners of the same.	[1896] P. 256.	Consistory Court of Norwich. T. C. Blofeld, M.A.		Confirmatory faculty granted for figures of Our Lord, St. Mary, and St. John on Chancel screen, on the ground that "there is, and has been, nothing in the services, or in the attitude of those who attend them, to indicate any probability of superstitious reverence being paid to these figures."

1896. Dec. 19.	*Vicar of Richmond and Chapelwardens of St. Matthias, Richmond v. All persons having interest.*	[1897] P. 70.	Consistory Court of Rochester. L. T. Dibdin, D.C.L.	Chancel *Gates* refused under *Bradford v. Fry.* Figures on chancel screen of *Our Lord on the Cross, St. Mary, and St. John,* under *Ridsdale v. Clifton.*	
1897. Mar. 18.	*Vicar and Churchwardens of Great Bardfield v. All having interest.*	[1897] P. 185.	Consistory Court of St. Albans. A. B. Kempe, M.A.		Faculty granted for restoration of stone figures of *Our Lord on the Cross, St. Mary,* and *St. John* on pre-Reformation stone Chancel screen extending from the ground to top of pointed Chancel arch, "the Ordinary being satisfied that the figures would be for the purpose of architectural decoration only, and that there was no ground for reasonable apprehension that they would be abused or made the subject of superstitious reverence."
1897. Dec. 7.	*In re St. Mark's, Marylebone Road. Vicar of St. Mark's v. Parishioners of the same.* [Consolidated suits.]	[1898] P. 114.	Consistory Court of London. Dr. Tristram.	1. *Stations of the Cross* ordered to be removed. 2. *Crucifixes* over pulpit and on a box in centre of reredos ordered to be removed. 3. *Curtains covering Ten Commandments, Lord's Prayer, and Apostles' Creed* engraved on East wall of Chancel ordered to be removed.	New reredos and Holy Table, erected without a faculty, sanctioned on the ground that they were "artistically an improvement to the Chancel," provided that a box on the reredos "apparently constructed with a view to placing in it the Reserved Sacrament" were kept closed, and that the platform on which the Holy Table was placed were "extended round the North End of the Holy Table."

DATE.	NAME OF SUIT AND CHURCH.	REFERENCE.	COURT AND JUDGE.	POINTS DECIDED.	
				ILLEGAL.	LEGAL.
1899. Aug. 12.	Kensit v. Rector and Churchwardens of St. Ethelburga, Bishopsgate Within.	[1900] P. 80.	Consistory Court of London. Dr. Tristram.	*Crucifixes* over Holy Table and Pulpit. "They are in ecclesiastical law *ornaments and not architectural decorations*, and, not being in use . . . in the second year of Edward VI. as church ornaments, their introduction into a Parish Church is prohibited by the Ornaments rubric." "It is not competent to an Ecclesiastical Court to grant a faculty for the introduction into a church of an isolated crucifix as *an architectural decoration*. . ."	
1900. Aug. 16.	In re St. Anselm, Pinner.	[1901] P. 202.	Consistory Court of London. Dr. Tristram.	Faculty refused for Chancel screen with figures of *Our Lord upon the Cross, St. Mary and St. John*, under *Ridsdale v. Clifton*.	
1901. Mar. 11.	In re St. Anselm, Pinner.	[1901] P. at p. 212.	Court of Arches. Sir Arthur Charles (on appeal).		Faculty granted, relying on *Hughes v. Edwards*, and upon the principle laid down in *Phillpotts v. Boyd*, and "emphatically approved" in *Ridsdale v. Clifton*, as to abuse for superstitious purposes. No evidence of such abuse, actual or probable.
		p. 218.		*Remarks.* The learned judge based his decision on the fact that there was "nothing in the furniture or arrangements of	

1900. Aug. 21.	*Davey v. Hinde.* [Church of the Annunciation, Brighton.]	[1901] P. 95. Consistory Court of Chichester. Dr. Tristram.	1. *Stations of the Cross.* 2. *Confessional boxes*, "on the ground that they are not articles of church furniture, requisite for or conducive to conformity with the doctrine or practice of the Church of England in relation to the reception of confession." 3. *Holy water stoups.* 4. *Crucifixes.* 5. *Tabernacles* for the reception of the *Reserved Sacrament* on the Holy Table in the Chancel and side Chapel, before which a light was continually kept burning. 6. Images of the *Good Shepherd* with candles on each side of it, and a lighted lamp in front of it; the *Virgin Mary*, with candles on each side of it, vases of flowers, and a lighted blue lamp before it, and a curtain with a canopy, crown, and star over it; and images on either side of the Holy Table in the side Chapel representing the *Sacred Heart* and *St. Joseph.*

the church or in the mode in which the services are conducted to warrant" an inference as to any probability of abuse. "The information given to me . . . satisfied me that the law, both in regard to the services and in regard to the ornaments of the church and the minister, has always been loyally obeyed."

DATE.	NAME OF SUIT AND CHURCH.	REFERENCE.	COURT AND JUDGE.	POINTS DECIDED. ILLEGAL.	POINTS DECIDED. LEGAL.
1902. Aug. 6.	Dawey v. Hinde. [Case re-heard after Prohibition, and Bishop's consent to hearing obtained.]	[1903] P. 221.	Consistory Court of Chichester. Dr. Tristram.		Judgment of Aug. 21, 1900, adopted and re-affirmed, and faculty for removal of illegal ornaments ordered to issue.
1902. Feb. 25.	Brockman and others v. All of St. John the Baptist, West Derby.	Liverpool Courier and Liverpool Daily Post, of Feb. 26, 1902.	Consistory Court of Liverpool. Rev. T. E. Espin, D.D., D.C.L.	Confirmatory faculty refused for erection of crucifix on wall behind pulpit.	
1904. Mar. 30.	Rector and Churchwardens of St. Luke's, Chelsea v. Wheeler.	[1904] P. 257.	Consistory Court of London. Dr. Tristram.		Moveable Holy Table of marble. Holy Table of wood with front and sides covered with detachable frames of slate containing marble mosaics.
1904. Sept. 26.	Vicar and Churchwardens of Paignton v. All having interest.	[1895] P. 111.	Consistory Court of Exeter. C. E. H. Chadwyck-Healey, K.C.	Faculty refused for figures of Our Lord upon the Cross, St. Mary, and St. John, above the Chancel screen having on the top a platform, gallery, or loft approached by ancient rood stairs and rood loft door, on the ground that "the erection in the church of a pre-Reformation screen and rood in the identical positions occupied by them before the Reformation would, so far as related to the group of sculptured figures, be unlawful, or if not unlawful, be inexpedient."	Chancel gates allowed.

1906. Feb. 6.	Markham v. All and Singular the Vicar, Churchwardens, Parishioners, and Inhabitants of Shirebrook.	[1906] P. 239.	Consistory Court of Southwell. A. B. Kempe, M.A.	Confirmatory faculty granted for an image of the *Good Shepherd* standing on a bracket under a canopy about ten feet from the ground, made of oak and uncoloured, as not "in the least likely to give occasion for superstitious reverence in any form." *Remarks:* An appeal *apud acta* was asserted to the Court of Arches, but was discontinued.
				1. *Stations of the Cross* ordered to be removed as being "intended to take a place or play a part in devotions to be paid to the Deity before them," and having been in fact used as intended. 2. *Crucifixes over pulpits* ordered to be removed as being "such unusual adjuncts of the pulpits of churches of the Church of England, that they ought not to be authorised unless there be a very general desire for them on the part of the church-going parishioners." 3. *Sacring bell* and *altar card*, containing unauthorised prayers, by consent withdrawn from the church.
1906. May 28.	*In re Christ Church, Ealing.*	[1906] P. 289.	Consistory Court of London. Dr. Tristram.	*Figure of Our Lord* represented as standing and in the act of blessing, sculptured in stone in high relief, under life-size, about five feet high, and surrounded by a frame containing representations of angels, on a pedestal at east end of north aisle. Allowed as a representation of an historical event, set up for the purpose of decoration only.

DATE.	NAME OF SUIT AND CHURCH.	REFERENCE.	COURT AND JUDGE.	POINTS DECIDED. ILLEGAL.	POINTS DECIDED. LEGAL.
1906. June 14.	In re St. Mary's, Chester. Barber and others v. All of the Parish of St. Bridget with St. Martin's, Chester.	Times of June 15, 1906; Guardian of June 20, 1906.	Consistory Court of Chester. Rev. T. E. Espin, D.D., D.C.L.	Faculty refused for *crucifix in churchyard* on site of ancient churchyard cross.	
Aug. 2.	,, ,,	Guardian of August 8, 1906.	,, ,,		*Cross in churchyard* allowed, and faculty decreed on amended petition.

Plan of Westminster Abbey as prepared for the Coronation, August 9, 1902.

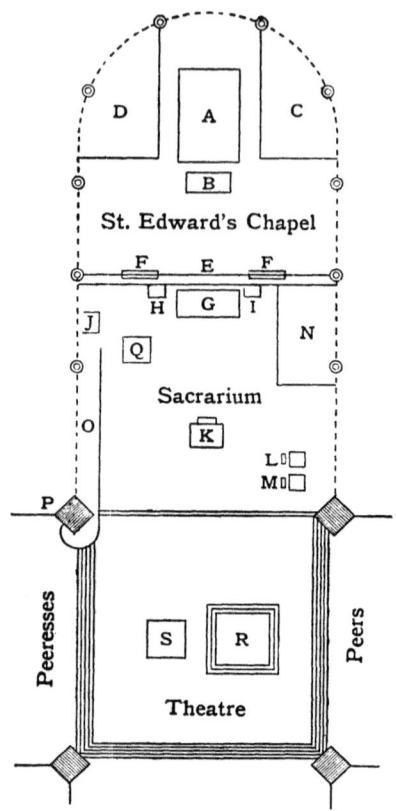

A.—Edward the Confessor's Shrine.
B.—Altar of St. Edward, on which the Regalia were deposited after the Service.
C.—King's Traverse.
D.—Queen's Traverse.
E.—Reredos.
F.F.—Doors through which the King and Queen passed to right and left into St. Edward's Chapel to be disrobed after the Service.
G.—High Altar.
H.—Archbishop of Canterbury's Chair, facing West.
I.—Position of Dean of Westminster.
J.—Archbishop of York's Chair.
K.—King Edward's Chair, containing the Stone of Destiny, facing the Altar.
L.—Chair and Faldstool, by which the King stood for the Recognition, and where he sate or knelt until the reading of the Gospel
M.—Chair and Faldstool for the Queen until her anointing.
N.—Places for the Prebendaries of Westminster and Great Officers of State.
O.—Bench of Bishops. The Archbishop of Armagh occupied the seat nearest the pulpit.
P.—Pulpit.
Q.—Faldstool, at which the Queen knelt to be anointed and crowned.
R.—King's Homage Throne, raised two steps above :—
S.—Queen's Throne after Crowning.

APPENDIX

THE CORONATION OF KING EDWARD VII. AND QUEEN ALEXANDRA

AUGUST 9, 1902

An Historical and Liturgical Account of the Ceremony

[This account of the Coronation of King Edward VII. and Queen Alexandra, in which special attention was paid to liturgical and historical exactitude, appeared in the *Westminster Gazette* of August 11th, 1902. It had the advantage of revision from personal knowledge and observation by Dr. Armitage Robinson, Prebendary (afterwards Dean) of Westminster on the day after the Coronation, and may be regarded as a faithful account of what actually took place. It is here reproduced by kind permission of the Proprietor of the *Westminster Gazette*.—C.Y.S.]

THE FORM AND ORDER OF CORONATION

I.—THE PROCESSIONS

The processions were formed in the temporary annexe outside the west door of the Abbey. On the King's right walked the Bishop of Durham,[1] on his left the Bishop of Bath and Wells,[2] vested in magnificent copes of white silk damask embroidered in gold. On the Queen's right walked the Bishop of Norwich,[3] on her left the Bishop of Oxford,[4] similarly vested. The paten was borne by the Bishop of Ely,[5] the chalice by the Bishop of Winchester,[6] and the Bible, on which the King was to take the

[1] Dr. Handley Moule.
[2] Dr. Kennion.
[3] Dr. Sheepshanks.
[4] Dr. Paget.
[5] Lord Alwyne Compton.
[6] Dr. Davidson.

oath, by the Bishop of London,[1] all vested in rich copes. The last-named three prelates immediately preceded the King. The Archbishops of York[2] and Canterbury[3] had places assigned to them according to their precedence in the State immediately in front of the officers bearing the Queen's Regalia. The King, with his attendants and supporters, followed the Queen, there being a pause of three or four minutes between the Queen's procession and the King's, which came last.

II.—Entrance into the Church and Recognition

Their Majesties, on entering, were received by the choir of Westminster singing the anthem, "I was glad when they said unto me, We will go into the house of the Lord," to music by Sir Hubert Parry. Passing up through the body of the church, under the nave screen, the Queen first and then the King were acclaimed, as they entered the choir, by the Westminster Scholars, occupying places in the Triforium above the organ on either side, who sang the words "Vivat Regina Alexandra!" "Vivat Rex Eduardus!" so arranged as to form part of Sir Hubert Parry's Anthem. The King's scholars of Westminster claim to represent the people of England at the Coronation, and there is evidence of their having exercised this right at every Coronation from the time of James II. According to the original order of service the King and Queen would have ascended the steps to the "Theatre"—a square platform which had been erected in the central space under the "Lantern"—from which the ceremony known as the "recognition" would have taken place. The procedure, however, was altered, in order to spare the King unnecessary fatigue, and they passed—The Queen with her supporters first, and then the King—straight to the chairs which had been placed for them in the Sacrarium, and the Recognition was performed once only, the Archbishop standing near King Edward's Chair and facing west. Near him stood the Lord Chancellor, the Lord Great Chamberlain, the Lord High Constable—The Duke of Fife—the Earl-Marshal, and Norroy King of Arms.[4] Then the Archbishop said in a loud voice:

"Sirs, I here present unto you King Edward, the undoubted

---

[1] Dr. Winnington-Ingram.   [2] Dr. Maclagan.
[3] Dr. Temple.   [4] W. H. Weldon, Esquire.

King of this Realm : Wherefore all you who are come this day to do your homage, are you willing to do the same ? "

Loud shouts of " God save King Edward !", started as before by the Westminster boys and taken up by the choir and the whole company, conveyed the required assent. The King at this time was still in the robe of crimson velvet with the ermine train in which he had made his entry, and which he retained until the Anointing. The Communion Service—the Litany having previously been sung by the Bishops of Bath and Wells and of Oxford at the entrance to Henry the Seventh's Chapel—was immediately begun by the Archbishop. It proceeded in the usual form save for the omission of the Commandments [which were not included in the service till the Coronation of George II.] and the insertion of a special Collect, removed from the place which it formerly occupied at the end of the Litany, instead of those for the King in ordinary use. The Epistle taken from 1 St. Peter, chap. 2, ending with the words, " Honour all men. Love the brotherhood. Fear God. Honour the King," was read by the Bishop of Ely. The Gospel, taken from the 22nd chapter of St. Matthew, containing the words, " Render therefore unto Cæsar the things which are Cæsar's : and unto God the things that are God's," was read by the Bishop of Winchester, all standing. The Nicene Creed was then sung to music by S. S. Wesley, all facing east.

III.—THE OATH

The King, who had now resumed his " cap of crimson velvet turned up with ermins," which he had removed for his private prayers, and, sitting to the right of the Queen in the chair already mentioned on the south side of the Sacrarium, prepared himself for the Oath, which, together with the long series of acts and ceremonies that make up " the Coronation," intervened between the first and the second part of the Communion Service. The Archbishop of Canterbury advanced to the King still seated in his chair, and, standing before him, said :

" Sir—Is your Majesty willing to take the Oath ? "

The King : " I am willing."

The Archbishop then administered three questions to the King, who, holding the book in his hand, duly and in a loud and clear voice returned the prescribed answers. The King then made his Solemn Oath, in the sight of all the people, laying his right hand upon the Holy Gospel in the Great Bible brought to him from the altar, and laid open at the Gospel of St. John, and tendered to him as he knelt, with these words: "The things which I have here before promised I will perform and keep. So help me God." The King then kissed the book and signed the Oath, using a silver standish (or inkstand) brought to him for the purpose.

IV.—THE ANOINTING AND VESTING

After taking the Oath, the King knelt at his faldstool beside the Queen during the singing of the hymn "Veni Creator Spiritus," of which the Archbishop said the first line.

The Archbishop then standing at the altar said the prescribed prayer, laying his hand on the Ampulla, a golden vessel in the form of an eagle, which contained the holy oil, previously "hallowed" by Bishop Welldon, Prebendary of Westminster, at the newly-erected altar in St. Edward's Chapel.

The choir then sang Handel's Coronation Anthem, "Zadok the priest and Nathan the prophet anointed Solomon king." [These words have been sung in this place for more than a thousand years.]

Meanwhile the King rose from his devotions and was disrobed of his crimson robes by the Lord Great Chamberlain, and, having taken off his cap of State, went and sat down in King Edward's [the First's] chair (containing the mystic stone) which had been placed in the Sacrarium near the western side, facing the altar. Norroy King of Arms, acting for Sir Albert Woods, Garter King of Arms, then summoned four Earls, Knights of the Garter (Lords Spencer, Derby, Cadogan, and Rosebery), who held over the King (to screen him) a rich pall of cloth of gold, delivered to them by the Lord Chamberlain. The King's undertunic or shirt of crimson satin contained the requisite opening in front for the anointing of the breast.

Everything being ready, the Sub-Dean of Westminster[1] (acting

---

[1] Dr. Duckworth.

at this and several other points for the Dean[1]) took the Ampulla and spoon (the only survivals of the original pre-Commonwealth Regalia, said to date from Edward III.) from the altar, and poured some of the holy oil into the spoon, and with it the Archbishop anointed the King in the form of a cross:

1. On the crown of the head, saying:
"Be thy Head anointed with Holy Oil, as kings, priests, and prophets were anointed."

2. On the breast, saying:
"Be thy Breast anointed with Holy Oil."

[This is a return to earlier usage. It exactly coincides with the form used at Richard I.'s and again at William and Mary's Coronation, and at later Coronations to George IV. inclusive. The anointing of the breast was omitted for William IV. and Victoria.]

3. On the palms of both hands, saying:
"Be thy Hands anointed with Holy Oil."

[The King's tunic or shirt was in earlier times then closed and fastened by the Dean of Westminster. This is not now necessary. The tips of the shoulders, the spaces between the shoulders, and the "bowings" of the elbows, also were at one time anointed. After the anointing the King's head was bound round the brows with a shallow coif of fine lawn which in the Middle Ages was not removed for eight days. A pair of linen gloves was put on after the anointing of the hands; but this custom was discontinued after James II.].

The Sub-Dean, having dried the places anointed with cotton-wool, in accordance with ancient usage, then laid the Ampulla and spoon upon the altar.

The King then knelt at his faldstool while the Archbishop, standing, said a prayer or blessing over him.

After this the King rose from his knees and resumed his seat in King Edward's chair, while the four Knights of the Garter gave back the pall to the Lord Chamberlain. The King then rose, and the Sub-Dean of Westminster put upon his Majesty the *Supertunica* or close pall of cloth of gold (said to represent the dalmatic or Eucharistic vestment of a deacon), together with a girdle of the same.

[1] Very Rev. G. G. Bradley.

[*Note.*—The *Colobium Sindonis*, a sort of alb of fine linen, which was in readiness, was not put upon the King, to spare His Majesty fatigue. It was omitted at the Coronation of William IV. also.]

V.—The Presenting of the Spurs and Sword and the Girding and Oblation of the Sword

Here followed a remarkable ceremony. The golden spurs were brought from the the altar, and with them the Lord Great Chamberlain touched the King's heels and then returned them to the Sub-Dean. Then came a most striking piece of ritual. Lord Londonderry who was bearing the Sword of State, exchanged this for another sword in a scabbard of purple velvet. This he handed to the Archbishop, who laid it with a special prayer upon the altar. Then the Archbishop of Canterbury, assisted by the Archbishop of York, the Bishops of London and Winchester, and other Bishops, went down and presented it to the King, saying :

"Receive this Kingly sword, brought now from the Altar of God, and delivered to you by the hands of us, the Bishops and servants of God, though unworthy." The sword was then girt upon the King by the Lord Great Chamberlain. The Archbishop then addressed this solemn admonition to him :

"With this Sword do justice, stop the growth of iniquity, protect the Holy Church of God, help and defend widows and orphans, restore the things that are gone to decay, maintain the things that are restored, punish and reform what is amiss, and confirm what is in good order : that doing these things you may be glorious in all virtue," &c.

[This is a return to earlier usage. William IV. was not girt.]

Then the King returned his sword to be laid on the altar as a solemn offering. The sword now belonged to the altar of the Abbey, and could not be removed until it was redeemed. Accordingly, Lord Londonderry came up and presented 100 shillings as the price of it, which the Sub-Dean received in a golden basin and placed upon the altar. Then he gave the sword back to Lord Londonderry, who drew it from its scabbard, and held it naked before his Majesty for the rest of the ceremony.

APPENDIX

VI.—The Investing with the Armilla and Imperial Mantle, and the Delivery of the Orb

The King then rose and stood while the *Armilla* (a kind of embroidered stole) and the Imperial Mantle or Pall of Cloth of Gold (in shape resembling a cope) were put upon him by the Sub-Dean of Westminster. [This pall was not put on William IV., but the Imperial Mantle of Purple Velvet (mentioned *infra*, p. 154) was used instead.] The King resuming his seat, the Orb with the Cross was brought from the altar and handed to the Archbishop, who delivered it into the King's right hand, with the words:

" Receive this Imperial Robe and Orb . . . . And when you see this Orb set under the Cross, remember that the whole world is subject to the Power and Empire of Christ our Redeemer." To free the King's hand the Orb was at once given back to the Sub-Dean, by whom it was laid upon the altar.

VII.—The Investiture per Annulum et Baculum

The Ruby Ring was then placed by the Archbishop on the fourth finger of the King's right hand with the words:

" Receive this Ring, the ensign of Kingly Dignity, and of defence of the Catholic Faith . . ."

The Sceptre with the Cross and the Rod or Sceptre with the Dove were then brought by the Dean to the Archbishop, the Glove presented by the Lord of the Manor of Worksop (the Duke of Newcastle) as the feudal service by which he holds his lands, being first put on the King's right hand. The Archbishop then delivered the Sceptre, with the Cross, into the King's right hand with the words:

" Receive the Royal Sceptre, the ensign of Kingly Power and Justice."

And the Sceptre with the Dove into the King's left hand, with the words:

" Receive the Rod of Equity and Mercy. . . . . Be so merciful that you be not too remiss; so execute Justice that you forget not Mercy. Punish the wicked, protect and cherish the just, and lead your people in the way wherein they should go." [This address has been slightly curtailed.]

VIII.—The Putting on of the Crown

The Archbishop then, standing before the altar, took the Crown into his hands and laid it again upon the altar. The Archbishop then pronounced a consecratory prayer in the following words :

"O God, the Crown of the faithful : Bless we beseech Thee and sanctify this Thy servant Edward our King : and as Thou dost this day set a Crown of pure Gold upon his Head "—here the King admonished by one of his supporting Bishops in accordance with the rubric, bowed his head—"so enrich his Royal Heart with Thine abundant grace, and crown him with all princely virtues, through the King Eternal Jesus Christ our Lord."

[This is an interesting return to the form used at the Coronation of James II., and is an improvement. At Charles I.'s Coronation the prayer here used, translated by Laud from older sources, was a blessing of the Crown, not the King.]

The King still sitting in King Edward's Chair, the Archbishop received the Crown from the Dean of Westminster, and reverently put it upon the King's head. This was the signal for loud and repeated acclamations of "God save the King !" ; the Peers put on their coronets, the trumpets sounded, the bells of the Abbey were rung, and at a signal the guns at the Tower and St. James's Park were shot off.

The Archbishop then delivered a brief exhortation beginning with the words, "Be strong and of a good courage," after which the choir sang the anthem, the "Confortare" of the ancient service, "Be strong and play the man : Keep the commandments of the Lord thy God, and walk in His ways," to music by Sir Walter Parratt.

[The *Confortare* was said by the Archbishop at the Coronation of Charles I. and subsequent coronations.]

[*Note*.—The crown used was the "Imperial Crown," which was again assumed by the King in his "traverse" after the ceremony. The so-called St. Edward's Crown was carried in procession but was not placed on the King's head.

IX.—The Presenting of the Holy Bible

The Sub-Dean then took the Bible from the altar and delivered it to the Archbishop, who presented it to the King with the words :

"Our Gracious King ; we present you with this Book, the

APPENDIX

most valuable thing that this world affords. Here is wisdom ; This is the Royal Law ; These are the lively Oracles of God." [This address has been much curtailed.]

[This ceremony was first introduced at the Coronation of William and Mary.]

The King returned the Bible to the Archbishop, who gave it to the Sub-Dean, by whom it was reverently placed upon the altar.

X.—The Benediction

The King having been thus anointed and crowned, and having received all the ensigns of Royalty, rose and went forward to his faldstool and there knelt while the Archbishop solemnly blest him with the words : " The Lord bless you and keep you : and as He hath made you King over His people so may He prosper you in this world and make you partaker of His eternal felicity in the world to come.

" The Lord give you a fruitful Country and healthful Seasons ; victorious Fleets and Armies and a quiet Empire; a faithful Senate, wise and upright Counsellors and Magistrates, a loyal Nobility, and a dutiful Gentry ; a pious, learned, and useful Clergy ; an honest, industrious, and obedient Commonalty."

[At all previous Coronations since William and Mary there have been *five* blessings, but these are now reduced to *two*. In the earliest times they numbered *fifteen !* The second of those given above has been taken verbatim from the service for the Coronation of George III.] After each benediction the Bishops and Peers said, " with a loud and hearty voice, ' Amen.' "

The Archbishop, turning to the people, then pronounced a prayer and blessing over them.

XI.—The Inthronisation and Homage

The King was then "lifted up" into his throne, that is to say, he walked, " supported " by the Archbishops, Bishops, and Peers, to the theatre and was placed in the great throne under the lantern. The Archbishop then knelt and did his homage, all the Bishops kneeling at the same moment and repeating the words with him. He then rose and kissed the King on his left cheek. The Archbishop found much difficulty in rising, and the King directed the Bishop of Bath and Wells to go to his assistance, and at the same time grasped the Archbishop's hand to help him. The Prelates in their robes, kneeling before the King, made a notable and picturesque group, but the Archbishop seemed to be much exhausted, and was with difficulty helped down the steps and back to his chair. Then followed the Prince of Wales and the Princes of the blood, all of whom first knelt before the King and swore their fealty in the prescribed words, then touched the crown on his Majesty's head, and finally kissed him on the left cheek. The senior Peers of each order followed with the same ceremony. During the homage of the Peers the anthem " Kings shall see and arise, princes also shall worship. . . . Behold these shall come from far ; and lo, these from the north and from the west ; and these from the land of Sinim " was sung to music composed for the occasion by Sir Frederick Bridge. [The homage was much curtailed to save time, and to spare the King fatigue.]

XII.—The Queen's Coronation by the Archbishop of York

The Queen then rose from her seat on the south side of the Sacrarium, and, with her trainbearers, went to the altar, supported by the Bishops of Norwich and Oxford, and there knelt down. The Archbishop of York meanwhile had left his place on the north of the altar and advanced to the Queen's faldstool, where he read a prayer for the Queen containing the words :

"Multiply Thy blessings upon this Thy servant, whom in Thy Name with all humble devotion we consecrate our Queen ; Defend her evermore from dangers, ghostly and bodily ; Make her a great example of virtue and piety, and a blessing to this kingdom."

Her Majesty continued kneeling at the faldstool before the altar between the steps and King Edward's Chair. Four Peeresses, summoned by Norroy King of Arms, held a rich pall of cloth of gold over her, while the Archbishop of York poured some of the holy oil upon the crown of her head with the words :

" In the Name of the Father, and of the Son, and of the Holy Ghost : Let the anointing with this Oil increase your honour, and the grace of God's Holy Spirit establish you, for ever and ever."

[A prayer used after this at the Coronation of Queen Adelaide and other Queens Consort was omitted.]

The Archbishop of York then put the Ruby Ring upon the fourth finger of the Queen's right hand with the words :

" Receive this Ring, the seal of a sincere Faith," &c. The Archbishop then received the Crown from the Altar and reverently set it upon the Queen's Head with the words :

"Receive the Crown of glory, honour, and joy; and God the Crown of the faithful, who by our Episcopal hands (though unworthy) doth this day set a Crown of pure Gold upon your Head enrich your Royal Heart with His abundant grace, and crown you with all princely virtues in this life, and with an everlasting Crown of glory in the life which is to come."

The Queen being crowned, all the Peeresses put on their Coronets.

The Archbishop then placed the Sceptre in the Queen's right hand and the Ivory Rod with the Dove in her left, with the prayer:

"O Lord, the Giver of all perfection: Grant unto this Thy servant Alexandra our Queen that, by the powerful and mild influence of her piety and virtue, she may adorn the high dignity which she hath obtained."

The Queen then rose from her knees and, supported by her two Bishops as before, ascended the theatre, "bowing herself reverently" to the King as she passed him on his throne, and took her seat on the throne provided for her on his left.

[*Note.*—Several things are to be noted :
1. The Queen Consort is anointed on the Head only.
2. The sign of the Cross is not enjoined by the rubric.
3. She is crowned and anointed kneeling; the King sitting.
4. She does not receive the Orb.
5. No special Coronation robes are put upon her.
6. The accompanying prayers are entirely different from those used for the King, *e.g.*, she receives the ring as "the seal of a sincere Faith," while the King receives it as the "Ensign of Kingly dignity and of Defence of the Catholic Faith." The reason for the difference is largely that the form for the Queen represents an older stage historically—*e.g.*, the *pouring* of the oil on the head, which belongs to the single anointing; also the giving of the sceptres *after*, not before, the crowning. The Queen's form having been used less often has been less changed, and is more primitive. The Archbishop of York does not crown the Queen Consort as of right, as has been sometimes asserted. He crowned Her Majesty by grace of the King and with the consent of the Archbishop of Canterbury. The Queen Consort is not crowned as of right. Queen Caroline was excluded from Westminster Abbey at the Coronation of George IV. in 1821 by order of the King.]

XIII.—The Oblation and Communion

The Communion Service then proceeded with the offertory sentences, and a beautiful and ancient *offertorium*, "Let my prayer come up into Thy presence as incense: and let the lifting up of my hands be as an evening sacrifice"—used at the Coronation of Charles I., but omitted at the coronations of William IV. and Victoria—was sung to music by Purcell. Meanwhile, the King and Queen descended from their thrones to make their oblations. Delivering their sceptres to the Noblemen appointed to hold them, they went to the steps of the altar, and taking off their Crowns, which they delivered to the Lord Great Chamberlain and another appointed officer to hold, they knelt down. The Bread and Wine for the Communion were then brought from St. Edward's Chapel by the Bishops of Ely and Winchester, who delivered the paten and chalice containing them successively into the King's hands. The King then offered these Elements to the Archbishop of Canterbury, who reverently placed them on the altar with an appropriate prayer, and then, as the rubric directs, "decently covered them with a fair linen cloth."

The King, still kneeling, then made his oblations of a Pall or altar-cloth and an Ingot or Wedge of Gold, delivered to him by the Lord Great Chamberlain, which the Archbishop received and placed upon the altar. The Queen also in like manner made her oblations of a Pall or altar-cloth and a Mark-weight of Gold.

Their Majesties then returned to their chairs facing the altar and knelt at their faldstools while the Archbishop read the Prayer for the Church Militant and the rest of the Communion Service to the end of the Prayer of Consecration. The music of the "Sanctus" was taken from Stainer's Service in A. The Archbishop of Canterbury, having first received the Communion himself, communicated the Dean of Westminster. Then, followed by the Dean with the Cup, he communicated the Archbishop of York. The Archbishop of Canterbury then administered the Bread to the King first, then to the Queen, and the Dean of Westminster administered the Cup.

The King and Queen then put on their Crowns, took their sceptres in their hands again, and so remained until the end of the service.

The Post-Communion was said by the Archbishop and the "Gloria in Excelsis" was sung by the choir to music by Sir John Stainer.

The Archbishop pronounced the Benediction, all kneeling, and the service closed with a threefold "Amen" by Orlando Gibbons.

[*Note.*—This oblation has been displaced from the position which it occupied at all previous Coronations. Formerly there were two oblations, the Pall and Ingot of Gold at the beginning of the ceremony immediately after the Recognition. The Second Oblation of a Mark or Purse of Gold took place in the Communion where the combined oblation now stands. The appropriate prayers have been omitted. This curtailment of the oblations has been much criticised, as the First Oblation after the Recognition at the beginning of the service was a beautiful and dignified ceremony. No doubt the object was to save time.

George III. is sometimes said to have been the first King to remove his crown before receiving the Communion, but from the accounts it is clear that Charles II. did the same.

Down to the Coronation of George IV. a "towell of white silk" was held by two Bishops before the King while he communicated, a relic of the old "Houseling Cloth," which survives at St. Mary's, Oxford, Wimborne Minster, and in one or two other churches in England.]

XIV.—The Te Deum and the Recess

The *Te Deum*, which, for the shortening of the ceremony, had been removed from an earlier place in the service, was now sung (to Dr. Stanford's music), and formed an appropriate close. Meanwhile the King, attended and accompanied as before, the four swords being carried before him, rose from his chair, crowned and carrying his sceptre and rod. He passed through the door on the right of the altar into St. Edward's Chapel, the Queen at the same time passing into the chapel by the door on the left. As they passed, the Sub-Dean of Westminster delivered the rest of the regalia, the orb, spurs, &c., to the lords appointed to carry them. The Archbishop of Canterbury had meanwhile entered St. Edward's Chapel, where an altar had been prepared for the reception of the regalia at the foot of St. Edward's shrine. The King, standing before the altar, delivered the Sceptre with the Dove to be laid upon the altar. The Golden Spurs and St. Edward's staff were handed to the Sub-Dean of Westminster and by him laid there also.

The King went into his traverse and was there disrobed of his Imperial Mantle or Robe of State, and still wearing his other

Coronation vestments (the dalmatic, the stole, and girdle) was arrayed by the Lord Great Chamberlain in his Royal Robe of Purple Velvet. The Sceptre with the Cross was again placed in his right hand; and afterwards he received the Orb in his left.

The Queen, being arrayed in her Royal Robe of Purple Velvet, received the Sceptre with the Cross in her right hand and the Ivory Rod with the Dove in her left.

Thus attired the King and Queen proceeded through the Sacrarium and Choir to the West door of the Nave and left the Abbey.

[*Note.*—In St. Edward's Chapel "traverses," or dressing-rooms, had been curtained off for the use of the King and Queen. Some parts of the ceremonial, which it was the duty of the Dean of Westminster, Dr. Bradley, to perform, were, on account of the Dean's great age, and to spare him fatigue, performed by the Sub-Dean, Dr. Duckworth, while the Dean sat in a chair placed for him at the South end of the altar. Although the Archbishop of Canterbury had experienced so much difficulty in returning from the ceremony of the homage, his voice sounded as strong as ever, when he afterwards proceeded in the Communion Service. He still moved with such evident infirmity as to cause anxiety to those who were near him; but the fact is that his Grace, though tired, was by no means exhausted at the close, and that the rumour of his having nearly fainted was entirely due to the difficulty experienced in rising from his knees and descending the steps of the theatre.

The ecclesiastical portion of the ceremony, apart from the processions at entrance and departure, occupied exactly an hour and a half. This abbreviation was achieved almost entirely by the promptness with which the various acts were made to follow one another, as the result of careful and repeated rehearsals. Scarcely anything at all was omitted, except the Litany and the Sermon, which, in the form as originally prepared for June 26, was to have been delivered by the Bishop of London. The Litany, which in some form has been used for a thousand years on these occasions, was sung by the two Litany Bishops (Bath and Wells, and Oxford), and the Choirs of Westminster and the Chapel Royal, at the entrance of Henry VII.'s Chapel, during the course of the preliminary Procession of the Regalia.]

www.ingramcontent.com/pod-product-compliance
Lightning Source LLC
Chambersburg PA
CBHW060819190426
43197CB00038B/2147